Pocket
FLORENCE & TUSCANY

TOP SIGHTS • LOCAL LIFE • MADE EASY

**Virginia Maxwell,
Nicola Williams**

In This Book

QuickStart Guide

Your keys to understanding the city – we help you decide what to do and how to do it

Need to Know
Tips for a smooth trip

Neighbourhoods
What's where

Explore Florence & Tuscany

The best things to see and do, neighbourhood by neighbourhood

Top Sights
Make the most of your visit

Local Life
The insider's city

The Best of Florence & Tuscany

The city's highlights in handy lists to help you plan

Best Walks
See the city on foot

Florence & Tucany's Best...
The best experiences

Survival Guide

Tips and tricks for a seamless, hassle-free city experience

Getting Around
Travel like a local

Essential Information
Including where to stay

Our selection of the city's best places to eat, drink and experience:

◉ **Sights**

✖ **Eating**

🥤 **Drinking**

⭐ **Entertainment**

🔒 **Shopping**

These symbols give you the vital information for each listing:

☏ Telephone Numbers
⊙ Opening Hours
P Parking
⊖ Nonsmoking
@ Internet Access
🛜 Wi-Fi Access
🌱 Vegetarian Selection
🍴 English-Language Menu
👪 Family-Friendly
🐾 Pet-Friendly
🚌 Bus
⛴ Ferry
🚊 Tram
🚆 Train

Find each listing quickly on maps for each neighbourhood:

Bar Hemingway

16 🥤 Map p233, B2

Legend has it that Hemi self, wielding a machine erate this timber-pan ered bar during showpiece is a en by Papa ar town. Dress s.com; Hôtel Rit ⊙6.30pm-2a

---

Lonely Planet's city

Lonely Planet Pocket Guides are designed to get you straight to the heart of the city.

Inside you'll find all the must-see sights, plus tips to make your visit to each one really memorable. We've split the city into easy-to-navigate neighbourhoods and provided clear maps so you'll find your way around with ease. Our expert authors have searched out the best of the city: walks, food, nightlife and shopping, to name a few. Because you want to explore, our 'Local Life' pages will take you to some of the most exciting areas to experience the real city.

And of course you'll find all the practical tips you need for a smooth trip: itineraries for short visits, how to get around, and how much to tip the guy who serves you a drink at the end of a long day's exploration.

It's your guarantee of a really great experience.

Our Promise

You can trust our travel information because Lonely Planet authors visit the places we write about, each and every edition. We never accept freebies for positive coverage, so you can rely on us to tell it like it is.

The Best of Florence & Tuscany 157

Florence & Tuscany's Best Walks

Florence & Tuscany's Best...

Survival Guide 177

ANDREA PISTOLESI/GETTY IMAGES ©

QuickStart Guide

Welcome to Florence & Tuscany

Though surprisingly small, Florence (Firenze) is laden with cultural attractions and charm. Medieval streets evoke a thousand tales, and museums and churches safeguard the world's greatest repository of Renaissance art. Nearby destinations including Siena, Pisa, Chianti, San Gimignano and Lucca are similarly alluring, and are easily visited on day trips.

View of Florence
PETER ADAMS/GETTY IMAGES ©

Florence & Tuscany
Top Sights

Uffizi Gallery (p30)

Chock-full of Renaissance masterpieces, this Medici-built *palazzo* (palace) beside the Arno is home to major works by Giotto, Botticelli, Michelangelo, da Vinci, Raphael, Titian and Caravaggio.

Duomo (p24)

The polychrome marble facade and tapering *campanile* (bell tower) of the *duomo* (cathedral) are wonderful, but what makes this building so extraordinary is Filippo Brunelleschi's massive red-brick dome, one of the greatest architectural achievements of all time.

Basilica di Santa Maria Novella (p50)

Behind the magnificent green-and-white marble facade of this church lie extraordinary paintings, romantic cloisters and four stunning frescoed chapels.

Basilica di San Lorenzo (p66)

Parish church and mausoleum of the famous Florentine family dynasty, the Medicis, this Renaissance-era masterpiece was designed by Brunelleschi. Michelangelo contributed to its adjoining library and sculpture-filled Cappelle Medicee (Medici Chapel).

Museo del Bargello (p84)

Surprisingly ignored by the tourist masses, this museum housed in the city's oldest public building safeguards Italy's most comprehensive collection of Tuscan Renaissance sculpture, including major works by Donatello and Michelangelo.

Palazzo Pitti (p100)

There's almost an embarrassment of riches here, including 16th- to 18th-century art in the Galleria Palatina and 18th- and 19th-century art in the Galleria d'Arte Moderna, plus the atmospheric Giardino di Boboli (Boboli Garden).

PETER BARRITT/GETTY IMAGES ©

Galleria dell'Accademia (p64)

CESAR LUCAS ABREU/GETTY IMAGES ©

Home to the world's most famous statue – Michelangelo's *David* – the Accademia also holds the same sculptor's enigmatic and moving *Prigioni* ('Prisoners' or 'Slaves') and unfinished *San Matteo* (St Matthew).

Palazzo Vecchio (p34)

Presiding over the city's most atmospheric piazza is this medieval fortress palace, once home to the Medicis and now a repository of art by Michelangelo, Vasari, Donatello and Bronzino.

Basilica di Santa Croce (p86)

Its magnificent neo-Gothic facade, tombs of prominent Florentines (including Dante and Galileo) and frescoes by Giotto and his school make this one of the city's most notable churches.

Opera della Metropolitana di Siena (p138)

Arranged around Siena's *duomo,* one of Italy's most significant Gothic cathedrals, this cluster of ecclesiastical buildings includes a museum, baptistry and crypt all adorned with extraordinary art. (*Duomo,* Siena)

Museo Civico, Siena (p142)

Housed in a gloriously Gothic *palazzo* on Siena's signature piazza, Il Campo, this civic museum showcases a unique collection of secular and religious frescoes painted between the 14th and 19th centuries. (Fresco detail, Simone Martini)

Piazza dei Miracoli, Pisa (p126)

A huge urban carpet on which a group of exquisite Romanesque buildings are set, Pisa's 'Field of Miracles' is one of Italy's major tourist drawcards. Climb the famously leaning tower to truly appreciate its magnificence.

Florence & Tuscany Local Life

Insider tips to help you find the real city

Florence's 360,000 residents enjoy a lifestyle that is crammed with culture, backdropped by history and anchored by family, faith and food. Head to their neighbourhoods, churches, cafes and restaurants to see what makes life here so special.

A Day in Fiesole
(p80)

▶ Breathtaking views
▶ Historic buildings

Suspended in the hills above Florence, this tranquil village melds its historical attractions (Etruscan temple, Roman baths and theatre, medieval churches, Renaissance villas) with panoramic views and popular restaurants and bars. The result is a perfect day-tripper destination.

A Night Out in Santa Croce
(p88)

▶ Bars and clubs
▶ Restaurants galore

Head to the buzzing streets surrounding Piazza di Santa Croce and Piazza Sant'Ambrogio to eat, drink and be merry, Florentine-style.

Gardens of Florence (p104)

▶ Privately owned gardens
▶ Huge public parks

Space is at a premium in the historic centre, which is why locals are so passionately attached to the parks and gardens that tumble down the hillsides southeast of the Ponte Vecchio. Spend a day avoiding museum queues and embracing the sunshine.

City of Artisans (p114)

▶ Artisans workshops
▶ Designer boutiques

Given a choice, local shoppers always opt for artisan-created goods. So it's lucky that in the Oltrano neighbourhood, generations of family-run *botteghe* (workshops) work hard to ensure that the tag 'Fiorentina' lives up to its reputation as an international label of quality assurance.

Roman amphitheatre, Fiesole (p81)

Artist, Oltrarno (p114)

Other great places to experience the city like a local:

Florence & Tuscany
Day Planner

Day One

☀ With only one day, you'll need to get cracking! Head to **Piazza della Repubblica** (p40) for a caffeine hit at **Gilli** (p45) or one of its historic siblings, then make your way to the **Uffizi Gallery** (p30) for a masterpiece-driven introduction to Renaissance art. For lunch, join the city's fashionistas at **Gucci Museo Caffè** (p45) or grab a gourmet sandwich at **'Ino** (p43).

☀ Piazza del Duomo is your next stop. Climb to the top of the dome or the *campanile* (bell tower; only masochists need do both), marvel at the interior of the **duomo** (cathedral; p24) and *battistero* (baptistry), and admire the original *Door of Paradise* at the Grande Museo del Duomo.

☽ After all this, you'll deserve a drink and a meal. Saunter over the **Ponte Vecchio** (p118), admiring the sunset view from its central belvederes, and then choose between **Le Volpi e l'Uva** (p110) and **Il Santino** (p122) for your *aperitivo* (pre-dinner drinks accompanied by cocktail snacks). For dinner, sample Modern Tuscan cuisine at **iO Osteria Personale** (p119).

Day Two

☀ The **Basilica di Santa Maria Novella** (p50) is your first destination of the day. Be sure to look behind the altar to discover Domenico Ghirlandaio's vivid frescoes in the Cappella Maggiore, and go to the Cappellone degli Spagnoli (Spanish Chapel) to admire Andrea di Bonaiuto's monumental fresco cycle. Afterwards, enjoy a cup of tea in the genteel surrounds of the **Officina Profumo-Farmaceutica di Santa Maria Novella** (p61).

☀ San Lorenzo is your next stop. Duck past the market stalls to visit the **basilica** (p66) and then head around the corner to admire Michelangelo works and Medici conceit in the **Cappelle Medicee** (p70). For lunch, sit with the stall-holders at **Trattoria Mario** (p73) or munch on a *panino con bollito* (hefty boiled-beef bun) at **Da Nerbone** (p75) in the Mercato Centrale (Central Market). Afterwards, join the queue of Michelangelo devotees waiting to come face-to-face with *David* at the **Galleria dell'Accademia** (p64).

☽ As the sun goes down, head to Santa Croce and follow our **local life itinerary** (p88) to make the most of this hipster hotspot.

Short on time?
We've arranged Florence & Tuscany's must-sees into these day-by-day itineraries to make sure you see the very best of the city in the time you have available.

Day Three

Devote the morning to exploring the museums in **Palazzo Pitti** (p100), the **Giardino di Boboli** (p104) and the **Giardino Bardini** (Bardini Garden; p105) – one ticket will cover them all. Exploration over, you'll be ready to relax over a traditional Tuscan lunch at **Da Ruggero** (p109) or a glass of wine with a snack at **Enoteca Fuori Porta** (p109).

You're in a city of artisans, so spend your afternoon following the **local life itinerary** (p114) of the same name. Visit boutiques and workshops, purchase handmade wares, marvel at the survival of age-old traditions and celebrate over an *aperitivo* in a converted hat-making workshop.

Stay this side of the river, dining by candlelight at **Il Santo Bevitore** (p119) and then take a moonlit wander by the Arno, stopping for an icy indulgence at **Gelateria Santa Trìnita** (p118) along the way.

Day Four

On your last day, consider seeing some more of Tuscany on a day trip, although Florence still has much to offer. Enjoy a coffee or decadent hot chocolate at **Caffè Rivoire** (p45) before crossing Piazza della Signoria and making your way to the **Museo del Bargello** (p84) to check out its peerless collection of Tuscan sculpture from the Renaissance period. For lunch, join the local crowds at **Il Giova** (p92) or **Osteria Il Buongustai** (p40).

It's your last afternoon, so some hard decisions have to be made. For your next destination, choose between the **Palazzo Vecchio** (p34), **Palazzo Medici-Riccardi** (p71), **Museo di San Marco** (p70) and **Basilica di Santa Croce** (p86). If you're lucky, you may have enough time and energy reserves to visit two.

Bid farewell to Florence over a glass or two of *prosecco* (Italian sparkling wine) while watching the sun set over the Arno at **La Terrazza** (p44), then kick on to a delicious dinner featuring Tuscan favourites at **L'Osteria di Giovanni** (p56).

Need to Know

**For more information,
see Survival Guide (p177)**

Currency
Euros (€)

Language
Italian

Visas
Not needed for residents of Schengen countries or for many visitors staying for less than 90 days.

Money
ATMs widely available. Credit cards accepted in most hotels and many restaurants; exceptions are noted in reviews.

Mobile Phones
Local SIM cards can be used in European and Australian phones. Other phones must be set to roaming.

Time
One hour ahead of GMT/UTC; clocks are put forward one hour during daylight saving time (late March to late October).

Plugs & Adaptors
Electrical current is 230V. There are two types of plugs: one has three vertically arranged round pins and the other has two horizontal round pins.

Tipping
Most visitors leave 10% to 15% of the bill for waiters if there's no service charge. Round taxi fares up to the nearest euro.

❶ Before You Go

Your Daily Budget

Budget less than €70
▶ Dorm bed: €20–40
▶ Gourmet sandwich: €4
▶ Coffee drunk at bar: €1

Midrange €70–200
▶ B&B double room: €100–200
▶ Trattoria meal: €35
▶ Aperitivo: €8

Top End more than €200
▶ Double room boutique hotel: €200 plus
▶ Coffee sitting at cafe terrace: €4
▶ Meal in upmarket restaurant €50

Useful Websites

▶ **Florentine** (www.theflorentine.net) English-language newspaper.

▶ **Turismo in Toscana** (www.turismo.intoscana.it) Official Tuscan tourism authority site.

▶ **Firenze Spettacolo** (www.firenzespettacolo.it) City entertainment guide.

▶ **Lonely Planet** (www.lonelyplanet.com/italy/tuscany) Lots of practical information.

Advance Planning

▶ **Three months before** For high or shoulder seasons book accommodation as far in advance as possible.

▶ **Two months before** If travelling in spring, book tickets for Maggio Musicale Fiorentino.

▶ **Two weeks before** Book tickets for the Uffizi and Galleria dell'Accademia online at Florence Museums (www.firenzemusei.it).

② Arriving in Florence

Two international airports service the region: Pisa International Airport (☎ 05 084 93 00; www.pisa-airport.com; Piazzale D'Ascanio) and Florence Airport (www.aeroporto.firenze. it). Thello sleeper train services from Paris arrive at Stazione Campo di Marte, and Toscana Mare services from Vienna arrive at Stazione di Santa Maria Novella (Piazza della Stazione) as do high-speed trains from Milan, Bologna, Venice and Rome. Both train stations are in central Florence.

✈ From Pisa International Airport

Destination	Best Transport
Piazza della Stazione	Train & bus

✈ From Florence Airport

Destination	Best Transport
Piazza della Stazione	Shuttle bus or taxi

✈ At the Airports

Pisa International Airport (PSA) Services and facilities include a left-luggage desk, tourist-information office, snack bars and shops. The train station is less than 40m from the terminal; buy your tickets at the information office in the arrival hall.

Florence Airport (FLR) Tourist information desk and snack bars. Exit the terminal and bear right for the taxi rank. The bus stop is outside the arrival hall.

③ Getting Around

Florence is mostly easily explored on foot, so tourists have little need to use the city's transport. Exceptions are the bus services to Fiesole and Piazzale Michelangelo (p180).

Siena and San Gimignano are easily accessed from Florence by bus. Pisa and Lucca are best reached by train. To explore Chianti you'll need a car.

Car & Motorcycle

There are strict ZTLs (*Zone a Traffico Limitato;* Limited Traffic Zones) in Florence, Siena, Pisa, Lucca and San Gimignano. If you drive in them you risk a fine of up to €200. Visit www. comune.fi.it for a map of Florence's ZTL.

In Florence, free street parking is available in Piazzale Michelangelo. Pricey (around €20 per day) underground parking can be found around Fortezza da Basso and in the Oltrarno beneath Piazzale di Porta Romana. For other towns and cities, see individual sections for details.

🚌 Bus

Buses and electric minibuses serve Florence, but are used by few tourists. Most start/terminate at the ATAF bus stops opposite the southeastern exit of Stazione di Santa Maria Novella. Tickets cost €1.20 and are sold at the ATAF ticket office adjoining the station. Buses to the region depart from the Sita bus station off Piazza della Stazione.

Taxi

In most Tuscan cities, including Florence, taxis can't be hailed in the street. Ranks are found close to train and bus stations; in Florence you can call ☎ 055 42 42 or ☎ 055 43 90.

🚆 Train

The Italian rail network **Trenitalia** (www. trenitalia.com) is modern and efficient, but doesn't cover all of Tuscany. Check its website for routes, timetables and ticket prices.

Florence & Tuscany
Neighbourhoods

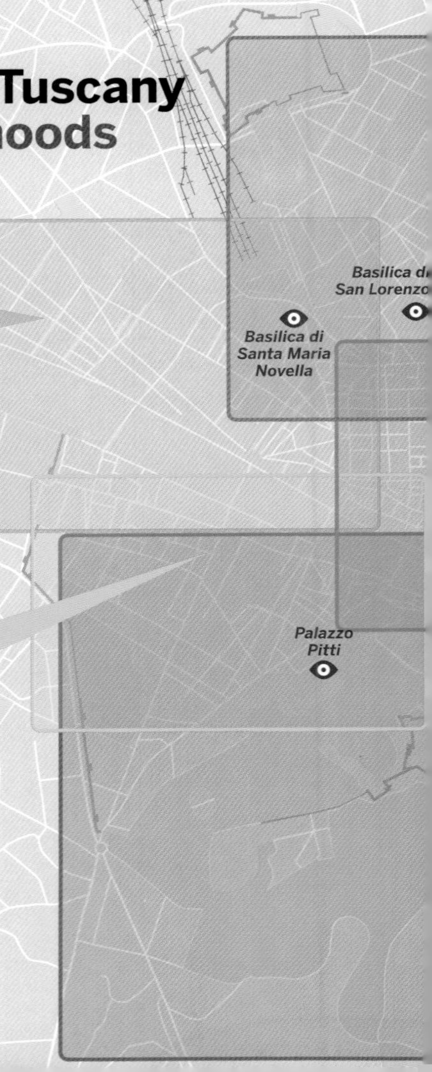

Santa Maria Novella (p48)

Shoppers have long been drawn to this chic corner of the city, lured by the sophisticated boutiques on Via de' Tornabuoni.

⊙ Top Sights

Basilica di Santa Maria Novella

Oltrarno (p112)

A beguiling labyrinth of cobbled streets and hidden piazzas sheltering traditional *botteghe* (artisans workshops), bohemian wine bars and foodie hotspots.

Worth a Trip
⊙ Top Sights

Piazza dei Miracoli (Pisa)

Lucca

Opera della Metropolitana di Siena (Siena)

Museo Civico (Siena)

Chianti

San Gimignano

Basilica di San Lorenzo

Basilica di Santa Maria Novella

Palazzo Pitti

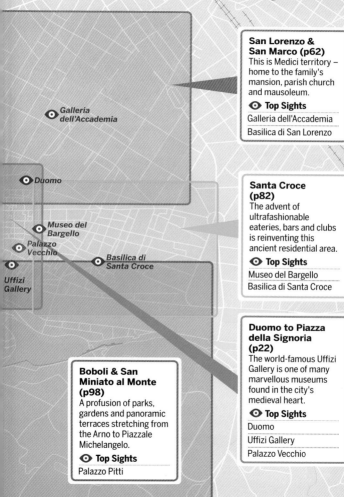

San Lorenzo & San Marco (p62)

This is Medici territory – home to the family's mansion, parish church and mausoleum.

⊙ Top Sights

Galleria dell'Accademia

Basilica di San Lorenzo

Santa Croce (p82)

The advent of ultrafashionable eateries, bars and clubs is reinventing this ancient residential area.

⊙ Top Sights

Museo del Bargello

Basilica di Santa Croce

Duomo to Piazza della Signoria (p22)

The world-famous Uffizi Gallery is one of many marvellous museums found in the city's medieval heart.

⊙ Top Sights

Duomo

Uffizi Gallery

Palazzo Vecchio

Boboli & San Miniato al Monte (p98)

A profusion of parks, gardens and panoramic terraces stretching from the Arno to Piazzale Michelangelo.

⊙ Top Sights

Palazzo Pitti

⊙ Galleria dell'Accademia

⊙ Duomo

⊙ Museo del Bargello

⊙ Palazzo Vecchio

⊙ Basilica di Santa Croce

Uffizi Gallery

Explore
Florence & Tuscany

Worth a Trip

Arno river, Florence
MAREMAGNUM/GETTY IMAGES ©

Explore

Duomo to Piazza della Signoria

Hub of the Renaissance and now the cosmopolitan heart of modern Florence, the tight grid of streets between the *duomo* (cathedral) and Piazza della Signoria packs one almighty historic and cultural punch. A neighbourhood harking back to Dante, the Romans and beyond, this is where the city's blockbuster sights – and most tourists – can be found.

The Sights in a Day

☀ Kick-start the day on Piazza della Repubblica with a quick breakfast at the Liberty-style bar in **Gilli** (p45), then walk to the Uffizi, pausing to admire the exquisite sculpted facade of **Chiesa e Museo Orsanmichele** (p38) en route. Devote the morning to world-class art at the **Uffizi Gallery** (p30).

☀ Walk to Piazza della Signoria for a light lunch on the terrace at **Gucci Museo Caffè** (p45). If fashion's your passion, visit the **Gucci Museo** (p38). Otherwise, dive straight into **Palazzo Vecchio** (p34), not missing the bewitching view from its tower. Devote the remainder of the afternoon to the city's iconic **duomo** (p24).

☾ Come *aperitivo* (pre-dinner drinks accompanied by cocktail snacks) hour, hit the river for a photogenic stroll along the Arno and its dusk-kissed bridges. Watch the sun set over a drink on the chic rooftop terrace of **La Terrazza** (p44), then walk west along Lungarno degli Acciaiuoli to shopping strip Via de' Tornabuoni where **Obikà** (p42) beckons for dinner.

◉ Top Sights

Duomo (p24)

Uffizi Gallery (p30)

Palazzo Vecchio (p34)

♥ Best of Florence

Eating

Osteria Il Buongustai (p40)

Cantinetta dei Verrazzano (p42)

Grom (p43)

'Ino (p43)

Drinking

Coquinarius (p44)

La Terrazza (p44)

Gucci Museo Caffè (p45)

Obikà (p42)

Le Renaissance Café (p45)

Caffè Rivoire (p45)

Gilli (p45)

Getting There

From Piazza della Stazione Walk southeast along Via de' Panzani and Via de' Cerretani and you will find yourself at the *duomo*. From here, Piazza della Signoria and the Uffizi Gallery are a short walk south down Via dei Calzaluoli.

Top Sights
Duomo

Properly titled the Cattedrale di Santa Maria del Fiore (Cathedral of St Mary of the Flower), but usually referred to as the *duomo* (another, often-used word meaning 'cathedral'), this magnificent building is the city's most iconic landmark. Designed by Sienese architect Arnolfo di Cambio, its construction started in 1296 and took almost 150 years. The result – distinctive red-tiled *cupola* dome, graceful *campanile* (bell tower) and breathtaking pink, white and green marble facade – has the wow factor in spades. Admission is free.

Cattedrale di Santa Maria del Fiore

◉ Map p36, E1

www.operaduomo.
firenze.it

Piazza del Duomo

🕒10am-5pm Mon-Wed & Fri, to 4pm Thu, to 4.45pm Sat, 1.30-4.45pm Sun

The Last Judgement fresco by Giorgio Vasari and Federico Zuccari

Don't Miss

Facade

The neo-Gothic facade was designed in the 19th century by architect Emilio de Fabris to replace the uncompleted original. The oldest and most clearly Gothic part of the structure is its south flank, pierced by **Porta dei Canonici** (Canons' Door), a mid-14th-century High Gothic creation (you enter here to climb to the dome).

Interior

After the visual wham-bam of the facade, the sparse decoration of the *duomo's* vast interior – 155m long and 90m wide – is a surprise. Most of its artistic treasures have been removed and those that remain are unexpectedly secular, reflecting the fact that the *duomo* was built with public funds as a *chiesa di stato* (state church).

Clock

Upon entering the *duomo,* look up high to see its giant painted clock. One of the first monumental clocks in Europe, it notably turns in an anticlockwise direction, counts in 24 hours starting at the bottom and begins the first hour of the day at sunset. The clock was painted by Florentine Paolo Ucello between 1440 and 1443.

Funerary Monument to Sir John Harkwood

Ucello painted one of the monumental equestrian frescos on the wall in the left aisle. Its subject, English military leader Sir John Halkwood, (1320–94) led Florentine troops to victory against Pisa in the Battle of Cascina (1364).

Dante's Divine Comedy

Near the dome ticket window (left aisle) hangs *La Commedia Illumina Firenze* (1465) by Domenico di Michelino. It depicts poet Dante

☑ Top Tips

▶ Dress code is strict: no shorts or sleeveless tops.

▶ Visit early in the morning to escape the crowds and avoid queuing in the sun.

▶ Tickets are valid for 24 hours (one visit to each sight) and can be purchased online at http://museumflorence.com or in person at the *campanile,* museum or Centro Arte e Cultura at Piazza San Giovanni 7.

▶ The most precious treasures from the buildings of the *duomo* group are stashed in the Grande Museo del Duomo (p29), an essential stop for all art lovers.

✗ Take a Break

▶ Enjoy lunch, dinner or a post-*duomo aperitivo* at Coquinarius (p44), a welcoming wine bar in nearby Via delle Oche. Or hit Tic Toc (p43), two doors down, for burgers Florentine-style.

▶ Head to Grom (p43) for some of the creamiest gelato in town.

Alighieri surrounded by the three afterlife worlds he describes in the *Divine Comedy:* purgatory is behind him, his right-hand points towards hell, and the city of Florence is paradise.

Mass Sacristy

Between the left arm of the transept and the apse is the **Sagrestia delle Messe** (Mass Sacristy). Its panelling is a marvel of inlaid wood carved by Benedetto and Giuliano da Maiano, and the fine bronze doors were executed by Luca della Robbia – his only known work in bronze. Above the doorway is his glazed terracotta *Resurrezione* (Resurrection).

Dome

When Michelangelo went to work on St Peter's in Rome, he reportedly said: 'I go to build a greater dome, but not a fairer one', referring to the huge but graceful terracotta-brick **dome** (combined ticket to dome, baptistry, campanile, crypt and museum adult/child under 14 €10/ free; ⏱8.30am-6.20pm Mon-Fri, to 5pm Sat) atop Florence's *duomo*. It was constructed between 1420 and 1436 to a design by Filippo Brunelleschi.

The Last Judgement

The most dramatic artworks inside the *duomo* are the flamboyant late-16th-century frescoes on the dome. Created by Giorgio Vasari and Federico Zuccari and covering an

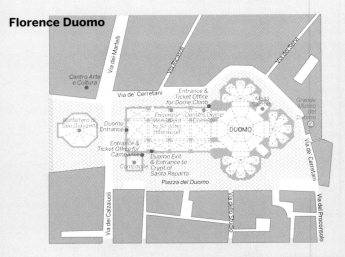

Florence Duomo

astonishing 3600 sq m, they depict the *Giudizio Universale* (Last Judgement). Look out for a spent Mother Nature with wrinkled breasts and the four seasons asleep at her feet.

Crypt of Santa Reparata

Stairs in the nave of the cathedral lead down to the **cripta** (crypt; combined ticket to dome, baptistry, campanile, crypt and museum adult/child under 14 €10/free; ⏱10am-5pm Mon-Wed & Fri, to 4pm Thu, to 4.45pm Sat), located in the excavated remnants of a basilica that stood on this site in the 5th century. Pay tribute to Filippo Brunelleschi, whose tomb is secreted among the stones, and check out the dome-inspired parasols in the souvenir shop, also (somewhat oddly) located here.

Campanile

Set next to the *duomo* is its slender **campanile** (bell tower; Map p36; combined ticket to dome, baptistry, campanile, crypt and museum adult/child under 14 €10/free; ⏱8.30am-6.50pm), a striking work of Florentine Gothic architecture designed by Giotto, the artistic genius often described as the founding artist of the Renaissance. The steep 414-step climb up the square, 85m tower offers the reward of a view that is nearly as impressive as that from the dome.

Bas Reliefs

Around the base of the *campanile*, the first tier has copies of the bas-reliefs

---

Understand
Scaling Brunelleschi's Dome
– – – – – – – – –

The most distinctive feature of the *duomo* (cathedral) is an extraordinary feat of engineering only fully appreciated by climbing its 463 steep interior stone steps.

Taking his inspiration from Rome's Pantheon, Brunelleschi arrived at an innovative engineering solution of a distinctive octagonal shape of inner and outer concentric domes resting on the drum of the cathedral rather than the roof itself, allowing artisans to build from the ground up without needing a wooden support frame. Over four million bricks were used, laid in consecutive rings in horizontal courses using a vertical herringbone pattern.

The balustrade at the base of the dome offers aerial views of the octagonal *coro* (choir) below, and seven round, stained-glass windows (by Donatello, Andrea del Castagno, Paolo Uccello and Lorenzo Ghiberti) pierce the octagonal drum.

The final leg – a straight, hazardous flight up the curve of the inner dome offering occasional snapshots of Florence through small windows – rewards with an unforgettable 360-degree panorama.

by Pisano depicting the Creation of Man and the *attività umane* (arts and industries). Second-tier reliefs depict the planets, cardinal virtues, arts and sacraments. Upper-storey niches are filled with 16 life-sized sculptures of pagan sibyls and the patriarchs, prophets and kings of Israel.

Battistero di San Giovanni

Across from the *duomo*'s main entrance is the 11th-century **baptistry** (Map p36; Piazza di San Giovanni; combined ticket to dome, baptistry, campanile, crypt and museum adult/child under 14 €10/free; 🕙11.15am-6.30pm Mon-Sat, 8.30am-1.30pm Sun & 1st Sat of month), an octagonal, striped structure of white-and-green marble with three sets of doors that tell the story of humanity and the Redemption. Dante is among the famous dunked in the baptismal font.

Baptistry's Doors

Andrea Pisano executed the baptistry's southern doors in the 1330s, illustrating the life of St John the Baptist. Lorenzo Ghiberti won a public competition in 1401 to design the northern doors, which show the life of Christ. The doors are copies; the originals are being restored.

Baptistry's Porta del Paradiso

Ghiberti's gilded bronze doors at the eastern entrance were created between 1425 and 1450 and dubbed the *Porta del Paradiso* (Door of Paradise) by Michelangelo. The panels illustrate scenes from the Old Testament. The doors are copies: the gleaming originals take pride of place in Grande Museo del Duomo.

Baptistry's Mosaics

The baptistry's interior gleams with Byzantine-style mosaics. Covering the dome in five horizontal tiers, they include scenes from the lives of St John the Baptist, Christ and Joseph on one side, and a representation of the Last Judgement on the other. A choir of angels surveys proceedings from the innermost tier.

Grande Museo del Duomo

Behind the *duomo*, this **museum** (Cathedral Museum; Map p36; www.operadu omo.firenze.it; Piazza del Duomo 9; combined ticket to dome, baptistry, campanile, crypt and museum adult/child under 14 €10/free; ⏱9am-6.50pm Mon-Sat, 9am-1.05pm Sun) is a repository of artistic treasures that once adorned the *duomo* and baptistry. The original Gate of Paradise panels are here, as are the sculptures that originally adorned the *Porta della Mandorla* (Almond Door) on the *duomo*'s north side.

Michelangelo's La Pietà

Just off the museum's stair landing is this wonderful piece, sculpted when Michelangelo was almost 80 (he intended it for his own tomb). Dissatisfied with both the quality of the marble and his work, the great man broke up the unfinished sculpture. It was later restored and completed by one of his students.

Top Sights
Uffizi Gallery

The Uffizi's extraordinary art collection spans the gamut of art history, but its core is the masterpiece-rich Renaissance collection – a morning can easily be spent enjoying its unmatched collection of Botticellis alone. The ongoing €65 million 'New Uffizi' project saw 1800 sq m of gallery space added in 2012 and expansion continues well into 2014. When complete (end date unknown), the Uffizi will include over 100 rooms and a designer exit by Japanese architect Arato Isozaki.

⊙ Map p36, D6

www.polomuseale.firenze.it

Piazzale degli Uffizi 6

adult/reduced €6.50/3.25

⊙8.15am-6.50pm Tue-Sun

Portraits of the Duke and Duchess of Urbino by Piero della Francesca

Don't Miss

13th-Century Sienese Art

Arriving in the **Primo Corridoio**, the first room to the left of the staircase (Room 2) is designed like a medieval chapel to reflect its fabulous contents: three large altarpieces from Florentine churches by Tuscan masters Duccio di Buoninsegna, Cimabue and Giotto. They show the transition from Gothic to nascent Renaissance style.

14th-Century Sienese Art

Room 3 moves into 14th-century Siena with Simone Martini's shimmering *Annunciation* (1333), painted with Lippo Memmi and setting the Madonna in a sea of gold. Note also Pietro Lorenzetti's *Madonna with Child and Saints* (1340).

International Gothic

In Room 4 savour the realism and extraordinary gold-leaf work of the San Remigio *Pietà* (1360–65) by Giotto pupil Giottino (aka Giotto di Stefano). The knockout piece in Rooms 5 and 6 – actually one large room – is Gentile da Fabriano's *Adoration of the Magi* (1423), originally commissioned for the church of Santa Trìnita.

Renaissance Pioneers

Perspective was a hallmark of the early-15th-century Florentine school (Room 7) that pioneered the Renaissance. One panel from Paolo Uccello's striking *Battle of San Romano* (1436–40), which celebrates Florence's victory over Siena, shows the artist's efforts to create perspective with amusing effect as he directs the lances, horses and soldiers to a central disappearing point.

Duke & Duchess of Urbino

Revel in the realism of Piero della Francesca's 1465 warts-and-all portraits of the Duke and

☑ Top Tips

► Cut out the queue: prebook tickets online (reservation €4) and collect on arrival.

► Allow time to linger in the 2nd-floor loggia or **Secondo Corridoio** (Second Corridor) linking the **Primo** (First) and **Terzo** (Third) corridors – views of the riverside and hills are intoxicating.

► Keep visits to three or four hours.

► To check the latest new rooms (and those temporarily closed during expansion works), go to the 'News' section of www.uffizi.org.

► Spot the closed door next to room 25 leading to the Medici's Corridoio Vasariano (p59), built to link the Uffizi with Palazzo Pitti (p100).

✗ Take a Break

► Head to the Uffizi's rooftop cafe for fresh air and fabulous views.

► Lunch on gourmet *panini* (sandwiches), wine and Tuscan chocolate at 'Ino (p43).

Duchess of Urbino (Room 8). The crooked-nosed duke lost his right eye in a jousting accident, hence the focus on his left side only, while the duchess is deathly stone-white to convey the fact that the portrait was painted posthumously.

Botticelli

The spectacular **Sala del Botticelli,** numbered 10 to 14 but really one large hall, is always packed. Of the 15 works by the Renaissance master known for his ethereal figures, *Birth of Venus* (c 1484), *Primavera* (Spring; c 1478) and deeply spiritual *Cestello Annunciation* (1489–90) stand out. Spot Botticelli's self-portrait (extreme right) in *Adoration of the Magi* (1475).

Leonardo da Vinci

Room 15 displays two early Florentine works by Leonardo da Vinci: the incomplete *Adoration of the Magi* (1481–82), drawn in red earth pigment (removed for restoration works at time of writing), and his *Annunciation* (c 1472), painted in Florence for the Chiesa di San Bartolomeo and moved to the Uffizi in 1867.

The Tribune

The Medici clan stashed away their most precious art in this octagonal-shaped treasure trove (room 18), created by Francesco I between 1581 and 1586. Designed to amaze and recently restored to its original exquisite state, it features a small collection

Uffizi Gallery

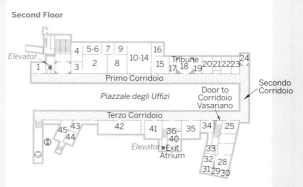

of classical statues and paintings on its upholstered silk walls and 6000 crimson-varnished mother-of-pearl shells encrusting the domed ceiling.

Tondo Doni
Michelangelo's dazzling *Tondo Doni,* a depiction of the Holy Family, hangs in room 35. The composition is unusual and the colours as vibrant as when they were first applied in 1504–06. It was painted for wealthy Florentine merchant Agnolo Doni (who hung it above his bed) and bought by the Medici for Palazzo Pitti in 1594.

Niobe Room
The huge Niobe Room (room 42) was built to house a group of 17 curvaceous, cream statues representing Niobe and her children. Discovered in a Roman vineyard in 1583 and brought to Florence in 1775, the works are 4th-century BC Roman copies of Greek originals.

Venetian Masters
Venetian masters grace Room 43, home to eight Titians. Masterpieces include the sensual nude *Venus of Urbino* (1538), and the striking portrait of *Eleonora Gonzaga, Duchess of Urbino* (1536–37). The next room, No 44, features works by Paolo Veronese and Tintoretto, the latter's famously ink-black *Portrait of a Man* (c 1555–60) is a moody highlight.

> ### Understand
> ## Palazzo degli Uffizi
>
> Cosimo I de' Medici commissioned Vasari to design and build the huge U-shaped Palazzo degli Uffizi in 1560 as a government office building (*uffizi* means 'offices') for the city's administrators, judiciary and guilds. Following Vasari's death in 1564, architects Alfonso Parigi and Bernando Buontalenti took over, Buontalenti modifying the upper floor to house the artworks keenly collected by Cosimo I's son, Francesco I, who inherited his father's passion for collecting. In 1580 the building was complete. By the time the last of the Medicis died in 1743, the family's private art collection was enormous. Fortunately, it was bequeathed to the City of Florence on the strict proviso that it never leaves the city.

Rembrandt to Raphael
Down to the 1st floor, the **Sala Blu** (Blue Room; rooms 46 to 55) displays 16th- and 17th-century works by foreign artists including Rembrandt, Rubens and Van Dyck. The next nine rooms showcase works by artists including Andrea del Sarto (rooms 56 to 59) and Raphael (room 66). Highlight: *Madonna of the Goldfinch* (1505–06), painted during Raphael's four-year sojourn in Florence.

Top Sights
Palazzo Vecchio

Plumb on Florence's most glorious square, this fortress palace with striking crenellations and 94m-high tower was the hub of political life in medieval Florence. Built for the *signoria* (city government) between 1298 and 1314, the 'Old Palace' played home to nine *priori* (consuls) – guild members picked out of a hat every two months. In 1540 Cosimo I commissioned Vasari to renovate and redecorate the upstairs apartments as his private residence, living here for nine years before moving to Palazzo Pitti.

◉ Map p36, D5

☑ 055 276 82 24

www.musefirenze.it

Piazza della Signoria

museum adult/reduced/child €10/8/free

🕙 museum 9am-midnight Fri-Wed, to 2pm Thu

Palazzo Vecchio

Don't Miss

Salone dei Cinquecento

Sheer size aside, what impresses about this 53m-long, 22m-wide salon are the swirling battle scenes painted floor to ceiling by Vasari and his apprentices. These glorify Florentine victories by Cosimo I over arch-rivals Pisa and Siena. Look up to see Cosimo portrayed as a god in the centre of the gold-leaf adorned panelled ceiling.

Chapel of SS Cosmas & Damian

Off the huge Salone dei Cinquecento is this chapel, home to Vasari's 1557–58 triptych of the two saints. Cosimo the Elder is depicted as Cosmas (right) and Cosimo I as Damian (left). Next to the chapel is the **Sala di Leo X**, the private apartments of Cardinal Giovanni de' Medici, son of Lorenzo Il Magnifico.

Studiolo

Cosimo I commissioned Vasari and a team of Florentine Mannerist artists to decorate this sumptuous study for his introverted, alchemy-mad son Francesco I (spot him disguised as a scientist experimenting with gunpowder in one of the 34 wall paintings). The lower paintings conceal 20 cabinets in which the young prince hid his treasures. Visit on a 'Secret Passages' tour.

Torre d'Arnolfo

On dry days (it's closed when raining), take a breathtaking, 418-step hike up this striking tower (admission €6.50) – the panorama of Piazza della Signoria and the city beyond is dazzling. Once up, you have 30 minutes to lap it up. No children under 6 years; and no more than 25 people on the terrace any one time.

☑ **Top Tips**

▶ Last tickets for the Torre d'Arnolfo are sold one hour before closing; in high season visit early morning or evening to avoid queues.

▶ Reserve guided tours (1¼ hours) in advance by telephone or email; the 'Secret Passages' tour is a perennial favourite and the 'Experiencing the Palace First-Hand' tour is perfect for families. Check the website for details.

▶ The *David* positioned outside the palace entrance is a copy (albeit on the spot where Michelangelo's original stood from 1510 until 1873); see the original at the Galleria dell'Accademia.

▶ Opening hours vary. See www.musefirenze.it for more information.

✖ **Take a Break**

▶ No hot chocolate is more famous, no pavement terrace more historic, than those at Caffè Rivoire (p45).

▶ The stylish Gucci Museo Caffè (p45) buzzes with local life and is a great option for lunch or a drink.

Grande Museo del Duomo

Via de' Cerretani

Piazza delle Pallottole

Piazza de S Benedetto

Via dello Studio

Via del Proconsolo

Chiesa di Santa Margherita

Via Santa Margherita

33 🚇

Duomo ◉

N

0   100 m
0   0.05 miles

Via della Canonica

Via delle Oche

19 ❌

15 ❌

Piazza Santa Elisabetta

Via Santa Elisabetta

Piazza del Duomo

Campanile

Via del Campanile

Piazza del Oglio

14 ❌

Via del Corso

Piazza de Donati

Via Dante Alighieri

10 🚇

Battistero di San Giovanni

Piazza di San Giovanni

Piazza del Adimari

Via dei Calzaiuoli

Via de' Cerchi

32 🚇

Via dei Cimatori

11 ❌

Via dei Magazzini

Piazza de' Cerchi

Via della Condotta

Via de' Cerretani

27 🚇

Piazza del Olio

Piazza dei Cavallari

Via Roma

Via de' Tosinghi

Via de' Medici

Via Speziali

13 ❌

18 ❌

Via dei Tavolini

Firenze Musei Ticket Window

Via Porta Rossa

Piazza di Santa Maria Maggiore

Via de' Pecori

Via del Campidoglio

Via de' Brunelleschi

25 🚇

8 ◉

Piazza della Repubblica

2 ◉

Chiesa e Museo di Orsanmichele

Via de' Lamberti

Via Arte della Lana

Via de' Conti

Via de' Vecchietti

Via degli Strozzi

Via Anselmi

Central Post Office

Via de' Sassetti

Via Pellicceria

Museo di Palazzo Davanzati

28 🚇

Piazza de' Davanzati

Via de' Banchi

Via de' Rondinelli

Via de' Agli

Via del Trebbio

Via de' Boni

Via Teatina

Via de' Pescioni

Piazza Strozzi

24 🚇

Via Monalda

Via de' Tornabuoni

Chiesa di San Gaetano

Via de' Corsi

Via de' Giacomini

12 ❌

26 🚇

Palazzo Strozzi

22 🚇

1 ◉

Via degli Strozzi

Sights

Palazzo Strozzi
ART GALLERY

1 ⊙ Map p36, A3

This 15th-century *palazzo* (palace) is one of Florence's most impressive Renaissance mansions. It was built for wealthy merchant Filippo Strozzi, one of the Medicis' major political and commercial rivals, and now hosts blockbuster art exhibitions. The contemporary art in its basement Strozzini gallery (free admission after 6pm Thu), stylish Le Renaissance Café (p45) and imposing internal courtyard are equally alluring. (www.palazzostrozzi. org; Via de' Tornabuoni; variable admission prices; ⊙10am-8pm Tue-Sun, to 11pm Thu)

Chiesa e Museo di Orsanmichele
CHURCH, MUSEUM

2 ⊙ Map p36, C4

This unusual church with a Gothic tabernacle by Andrea Orcagna was created when the arcades of a late-13th-century grain market were walled in and two storeys added during the next century. Its exterior is exquisitely decorated with niches and tabernacles bearing statues; these are copies – originals are in the church's light and airy upstairs museum, which is open only on Monday. (Via dell'Arte della Lana; admission free; ⊙church 10am-5pm, museum 10am-5pm Mon)

Museo Galileo
SCIENCE MUSEUM

3 ⊙ Map p36, D7

On the river next to the Uffizi is this state-of-the-art science museum, named after the great Pisa-born scientist invited by the Medici court to Florence in 1610. A visit will unravel a mesmerising curiosity box of astronomical and mathematical treasures collected by the Medici and Lorraine dynasties. (☎055 26 53 11; www.museogali leo.it; Piazza dei Giudici 1; adult/reduced/family €9/5.50/22; ⊙9.30am-5.30pm Wed-Mon, to 12.30pm Tue)

Museo Salvatore Ferragamo
MUSEUM

4 ⊙ Map p36, A5

The splendid 13th-century **Palazzo Spini-Feroni** has been the home of the Ferragamo fashion empire since 1938. Anyone with even the faintest tendency towards shoe addiction or interested in the sociohistorical context of fashion should not miss the esoteric but oddly compelling shoe museum. (www.museoferragamo.it; Via de' Tornabuoni 2; adult/reduced €6/free; ⊙10am-7pm)

Gucci Museo
FASHION MUSEUM

5 ⊙ Map p36, E5

Strut through the bookshop/store to reach this bijou museum, which tells the tale of the Gucci fashion house. Exhibits include the first luggage pieces in its signature beige fabric emblazoned with the interlocking 'GG'

GIORGIO COSULICH/GETTY IMAGES ©

Piazza della Signoria

logo, the 1950s equivalents in red-and-green stripe and even a gleaming white, 1979 Cadillac Seville with gold Gs on the hubcaps and Gucci fabric upholstery. (www.gucci.com; Piazza della Signoria 10; adult/child €6/free; ⊗10am-8pm)

Museo di Palazzo Davanzati

MUSEUM

6 ⊙ Map p36, B4

Tucked inside a 14th-century warehouse and residence that was home to the wealthy Davanzati merchant family from 1578, this *palazzo* museum with wonderful central loggia is a gem. Don't miss the 1st-floor **Sala Madornale** (reception room) with its painted wooden ceiling or the exquisitely decorated **Sala dei Pappa-**

galli (Parrot Room) and **Camera dei Pavoni** (Peacock Bedroom). (Via Porta Rossa 13; adult/reduced €2/1; ⊗8.15am-1.30pm, closed 1st, 3rd & 5th Mon, 2nd & 4th Sun of month)

Piazza della Signoria

PIAZZA

7 ⊙ Map p36, D5

Edged by historic cafes, crammed with Renaissance sculptures and presided over by magnificent Palazzo Vecchio, this photogenic piazza has been the hub of local life for centuries. Early evening and all day at weekends, Florentines indulge in the sacrosanct *passeggiata* (early evening stroll), breaking for a coffee, hot chocolate or *aperitivo*, perhaps at the city's

Local Life
Passeggiata

Nothing is more sacrosanct to Italians than the *passeggiata* (early evening stroll). In Florence, follow the lovely trail from the *duomo* (cathedral) to the city's most elegant square, Piazza delle Signoria. Or head to the upmarket shopping strip of Via de' Tornabuoni, prime terrain to don suitable dress and walk, chat and smooch in the chic company of Renaissance palaces and Italian fashion houses. Locals call the street the 'Salotto di Firenze' (Florence's Drawing Room).

most famous cafe, Caffè Rivoire (p45). (Piazza della Signoria)

Piazza della Repubblica   PIAZZA

8 ⊙ Map p36, C3

The site of a Roman forum and heart of medieval Florence, this busy civic space was created in the 1880s as part of a controversial plan of 'civic improvements' involving the demolition of the old market, Jewish ghetto and slums, and the relocation of nearly 6000 residents. These days it's best known for its historic cafes.

Loggia dei Lanzi   MUSEUM

9 ⊙ Map p36, D5

Home to sculptures such as Giambologna's *Rape of the Sabine Women,* Benvenuto Cellini's bronze *Perseus*

and Agnolo Gaddi's *Seven Virtues,* this loggia owes its name to the Lanzichenecchi (Swiss bodyguards) of Cosimo I, who were stationed here. The present-day guards live up to this heritage, sternly monitoring crowd behaviour and promptly banishing food or drink. (Piazza della Signoria; admission free)

Chiesa di Santa Margherita   CHURCH

10 ⊙ Map p36, E3

Dante fans will like to know that it was in this tiny 11th-century church, in the poet's old stomping ground, that he is said to have first espied his muse, Beatrice Portinari. And it is here that he ended up marrying Gemma Donati, to whom he had been promised. (Via Santa Margherita 4)

Eating

Osteria Il Buongustai   OSTERIA €

11 🍴 Map p36, D4

Run with breathtaking speed and grace by Laura and Lucia, this lunchtime favourite heaves with locals who work nearby and savvy students who flock here to fill up on tasty Tuscan homecooking at a snip of other restaurant prices. The place is brilliantly no frills – expect to share a table and pay in cash; no credit cards. (Via dei Cerchi 15r; meals €15; ⊙11.30am-3.30pm Mon-Sat)

Understand

Florentine Artists

In many respects, the history of Florentine art is also the history of Western art. Browse through any text on the subject and you'll quickly develop an understanding of how influential the Italian Renaissance, which kicked off and reached its greatest flowering here, has been over the past 500 years. Indeed, it's no exaggeration to say that architecture, painting and sculpture rely on its technical innovations and take inspiration from its humanist subject matter to this very day.

Of the many artists who trained, worked and lived in the city, the most famous are Giotto di Bondone (c 1266–1337), Donatello (c 1386–1466), Fra' Angelico (c 1395–1455), Masaccio (1401–28), Filippo Lippi (c 1406–69), Benozzo Gozzoli (c 1421–97), Sandro Botticelli (1445–1510), Domenico Ghirlandaio (1449–94) and Michelangelo Buonarroti (1475–1564).

The city is full of artistic masterpieces – in fact, Florence itself is often described as the world's biggest and most spectacular museum. It's impossible to see everything in one trip, but the **Uffizi Gallery** should be every visitor's first stop. Its peerless collection contains major works by every Renaissance artist of note, with Botticelli's *Primavera*, *Birth of Venus*, *Cestello Annunciation* and *Adoration of the Magi* being four of the gallery's best-loved works (Michelangelo's *Tondo Doni* is another).

Sculptures abound – most notably Michelangelo's *David* in the **Galleria dell'Accademia** – but the greatest and most significant concentration of works can be found in the **Museo del Bargello**, home to Donatello's two versions of *David* (one marble, the other bronze) and a number of works by Michelangelo.

Frescoing was an important artistic technique in the Renaissance, and Florentine churches are rich repositories of these murals painted on freshly laid lime plaster. Head to **Basilica di Santa Maria Novella** to see Ghirlandaio's wonderful examples in the Cappella Maggiore; the **Museo di San Marco** to see those of Fra' Angelico (including his deeply spiritual *Annunciation*); the **Cappella Brancacci** to see Masaccio's oft-reproduced *Expulsion of Adam and Eve from Paradise*; and the **Palazzo Medici-Riccardi** to admire Benozzo Gozzoli's charming *Procession of the Magi to Bethlehem*.

Obikà

CHEESE €€

12 Map p36, A3

Given its exclusive location in Palazzo Tornabuoni this designer address is naturally ubertrendy. Taste different mozzarella cheeses with basil, organic veg or sundried tomatoes in the cathedral-like interior or snuggle beneath heaters on sofa seating in the elegant, star-topped courtyard. The €9 *aperitivi* comprising a drink and twinset of tasting platters (mozzarella and proscuitto) is copious, as is Sunday brunch. (☎055 277 35 26; www.obika.it; Via de' Tornabuoni 16; 2/3/5 mozzarella €13/20/30, pizza €10-13.50; ☻noon-4pm & 6.30-11.30pm Mon-Fri, to 11pm Sat & Sun)

Cantinetta dei Verrazzano

BAKERY €

13 Map p36, D4

A *forno* (baker's oven) and *cantinetta* (small cellar) make a heavenly match. Sit down at a marble-topped table, admire prized vintages displayed behind glass-wall cabinets and sip a glass of wine (€4 to €10) produced on the Verrazzano estate in Chianti. The focaccia topped with caramelised radicchio is a must – as is a mixed cold-meat platter. (Via dei Tavolini 18-20; focaccia €2.50-3; ☻noon-9pm Mon-Sat, 10am-4.30pm Sun)

LONELY PLANET/GETTY IMAGES ©

Tripe cart

Tic Toc
BURGERS €

14 Map p36, D3

This stylish Florentine version of a US diner is worth a pitstop. Burgers are made from the finest handcut beef, chicken or veg, and homemade salsa and fries are a given. Food is served all day and the bar is an *aperitivi* hot spot. Jack Daniels anyone? (Via dell' Oche 15r; burgers €10, club sandwiches €7; ⊙11am-11pm Mon-Sat)

Grom
GELATO €

15 Map p36, D2

Slow food meets gelato. Top-notch ingredients including seasonal fruits make for remarkable gelato and *sorbetto* (sorbet). Try *crema di Grom,* a confection of cookies and chocolate. (www.grom.it; cnr Via del Campanile & Via delle Oche; ⊙10.30am-midnight Apr-Sep, to 11pm Oct-Mar)

'Ino
SANDWICHES €

16 Map p36, C6

Artisan ingredients sourced locally and mixed creatively by passionate gourmet Alessandro Frassica provide the secret behind this stylish sandwich bar near the Uffizi. Create your own combo, pick from dozens of house specials or go for a tasting platter (salami, cheese, *pecorini* – sheep's milk cheese). End with chocolate *degustazione* (tasting) – the one peppered with olive oil and lemon zest is sensational. (Via dei Georgofili 3r-7r; panini €8, tasting platter €12; ⊙11am-8pm Mon-Sat, noon-5pm Sun)

Local Life
Tripe Carts

When Florentines fancy food fast, they flit by a *trippaio* (tripe cart) for a tripe *panino* (sandwich). Think cow's stomach chopped up, boiled, sliced, seasoned and bunged between bread. *Trippai* still going strong include the cart on the southwest corner of the **Mercato Nuovo** (Map p36, C5) and the hole-in-the-wall **Da Vinattieri** (Map p36, E3; Via Santa Margherita 4; ⊙10am-7.30pm Mon-Fri, to 8pm Sat & Sun), down an alley next to Chiesa di Santa Margherita. Pay €4.50 for a tripe *panino* doused in *salsa verde* (pea-green sauce of smashed parsley, garlic, capers and anchovies) or around €7 for a bowl of *lampredotto* (fourth stomach, chopped and simmered).

La Canova di Gustavino
WINE BAR €€

17 Map p36, D4

The rear dining room of this atmospheric *enoteca* (wine bar) is lined with shelves of Tuscan wine – the perfect accompaniment to homemade black tagliolini in a seafood and pesto sauce or grilled quail with polenta and red radicchio crème brulée. Yes, cuisine is creative Tuscan and yes, one eats as well as drinks exceedingly well here. (☎055 239 98 06; Via della Condotta 29r; meals €40; ⊙noon-midnight)

Understand
Dante Alighieri

Italy's greatest poet was born in Florence in 1265 and spent his first 36 years here. Exiled in 1301 after a bitter power struggle within the ranks of the Florentine Guelphs (he was in the losing faction), Dante was never able to return home, a situation that he lamented greatly in his most famous work, the *Divina Commedia* (The *Divine Comedy*).

When Dante was just 12 he had been promised in marriage to Gemma Donati. But it was another Florentine girl, Beatrice Portinari (1266–90), who was his muse and – despite only meeting her twice in his life – the openly declared love of his life. In the *Divine Comedy,* Dante describes travelling through the circles of hell and purgatory, before finally meeting his beloved Beatrice in heaven.

Beatrice, who wed a banker and died a couple of years later aged just 24, is buried in the Chiesa di Santa Margherita. Dante died in 1321 in Ravenna, where he is buried.

I Due Fratellini
SANDWICHES €

18 Map p36, D4

This hole in the wall has been in business since 1875. Wash your *panino* down with a beaker of wine and leave the empty on the wooden shelf outside. (www.iduefratellini.com; Via dei Cimatori 38r; panini €3; ⏰9am-8pm Mon-Sat, closed Fri & Sat 2nd half of Jun & all Aug)

Drinking

Coquinarius
WINE BAR

19 Map p36, D2

This stylish *enoteca* has old stone vaults, scrubbed wooden tables and a modern air. The wine list features Tuscan greats and unknowns, and a substantial *crostini* (toasts with various toppings) and carpacci (cold sliced meats) menu ensures you don't leave hungry. Or stay for dinner – it's worth it. (www.coquinarius.com; Via delle Oche 11r; crostini & carpacci €4; ⏰noon-10.30pm)

La Terrazza
BAR

20 Map p36, B6

This rooftop bar with wooden decking terrace accessible from the 5th floor of the Ferragamo-owned Hotel Continentale is as chic as one would expect of a fashion-house hotel. Its *aperitivo* buffet is a modest affair, but who cares when that drop-dead-gorgeous panorama of one of Europe's most beautiful cities is on offer? Dress the part or feel out of place. (www.continentale.it; Vicolo dell Oro 6r; ⏰2.30-11.30pm Apr-Sep)

Slowly
LOUNGE BAR

21 🚇 Map p36, B4

Sleek and sometimes snooty, this lounge bar with a candle flickering on every table is known for its glam interior, Florentine Lotharios, and lavish, fruit-garnished cocktails – €10 including buffet during the bewitching *aperitivo* 'hour' (6.30pm to 10pm). Ibiza-style lounge tracks dominate the turntable. (www.slowlycafe.com; Via Porta Rossa 63r; 🕑9pm-3am Mon-Sat, closed Aug)

Gucci Museo Caffè
CAFE

Everything from the crockery to G-shaped sugar 'cubes' is emblazoned with the Gucci monogram, but the over-zealous branding can be overlooked at this smart, laid-back cafe, which is one of the city's hippest places (see **5** 🚇 Map p36, E5) to hang over coffee, lunch, *aperitivo,* newspapers, design books or inhouse iPads. A huge table hooked up with plugs makes it a laptop-user favourite. (Piazza della Signoria 10; meals €25; 🕑10am-11pm; 🛜)

Le Renaissance Café
CAFE

22 🚇 Map p36, A3

Soul-soaringly high vaulted ceiling, sleek black Panton chairs and exquisitely low drink prices seduce a mixed crowd at this artsy hangout in Palazzo Strozzi, plumb on Florence's most designer-chic street. The chocolate-swirled cappuccino (€1.40 sitting down) is among the best in town. (Piazza Strozzi; 🕑9am-8pm Fri-Wed, 9am-11pm Thu)

Caffè Rivoire
CAFE

23 🚇 Map p36, C5

The golden oldie in which to refuel after an Uffizi or Palazzo Vecchio visit, this pricey little number with unbeatable people-watching terrace has produced the city's most exquisite chocolate since 1872 – pay €6.50 (with whipped cream €8) for the privilege of enjoying one sitting down. (Piazza della Signoria 4; 🕑Tue-Sun)

Colle Bereto
LOUNGE BAR

24 🚇 Map p36, B3

The local fashion scene's bar of choice, Colle Bereto is where the bold and the beautiful come to see or be seen for breakfast, lunch or at *aperitivo* hour. (Piazza Strozzi 5; 🕑8am-2am Tue-Sun; 🛜)

Gilli
HISTORIC CAFE

25 🚇 Map p36, C3

The city's grandest cafe, Gilli has been serving excellent coffee and delicious cakes since 1733. Claiming a table on the piazza is *molto* expensive – we prefer standing at the spacious Liberty-style bar. (www.gilli.it; Piazza della Repubblica 39r; 🕑Wed-Mon)

Procacci
CAFE

26 🚇 Map p36, A3

The last remaining bastion of genteel old Florence on Via de' Tornabuoni, this tiny cafe was born in 1885 as a delicatessen serving truffles in its repertoire of tasty morsels. Bite-sized *panini tartufati* (truffle pâté

Local Life
Florence Fashion

Florence screams fashion. And there's no finer street on which to shop in this city synonymous with beauty, creativity and skilled craftsmanship than **Via de' Tornabuoni**, with its dazzling line-up of designers. Find everyone from Prada to Cartier here, as well as home-grown players Roberto Cavalli, Salvatore Ferragamo (with glittering shoe museum to boot) and Florence fashion icon Gucci (born in 1921 as a tiny saddlery shop around the corner on Via della Vigna Nuova).

rolls) remain the thing to order, best accompanied by a glass of *prosecco*. (www.procacci1885.it; Via de' Tornabuoni 64r; ☺10am-8pm Mon-Sat)

Fiaschetteria Nuvoli   WINE BAR

27 🍴 Map p36, C1

Pull up a stool on the street and chat with a regular over a glass of *vino della casa* (house wine) at this old-fashioned *fiaschetteria* (small tavern) a street away from the *duomo*. (Piazza dell'Olio 15r; ☺7am-9pm Mon-Sat)

YAB   NIGHTCLUB

28 🍴 Map p36, B4

It's crucial to pick your night according to your age and tastes at Florence's busiest disco club which is located behind Palazzo Strozzi, which has been around since the 1970s. Thursdays is

the evening the over 30s hit the dance floor – otherwise, the set is predominantly student. (www.yab.it; Via de' Sassetti 5r; ☺9pm-4am Oct-May)

Shopping

Pineider   STATIONERY

29 🔒 Map p36, C5

This exclusive stationer opened at here in 1774, and once designed calling cards for Napoleon. Order your own, or choose from a tempting range of paper products and elegant leather office accessories. (www.pineider.com; Piazza della Signoria 13-14r; ☺10am-7pm)

Angela Caputi   FASHION

30 🔒 Map p36, B5

The colourful resin jewellery of Angela Caputi, here since the 1970s, is much-loved by Florentines. Costume gems and jewels are her forté, shown off against one-of-a-kind women's fashion labels uncovered during her travels. (www.angelacaputi.com; Borgo SS Apostoli 42-46; ☺10am-1pm & 3.30-7.30pm Mon-Sat)

La Bottega dell'Olio   OLIVE OIL

31 🔒 Map p36, A5

This boutique has displays of olive oils, olive-oil products (the Lepo skincare range is particularly good) and platters made from olive wood. (Piazza del Limbo 2r; ☺10am-1pm & 2-6.30pm Tue-Sat)

Shopping on Via de' Tornabuoni

Fabriano Boutique STATIONERY

32 Map p36, D3

Luxurious writing paper and origami and pop-up greeting cards are amongst the paper products that entice customers into this thoroughly modern stationery boutique – a refreshing change from the traditional norm. It also organises card-making, calligraphy and origami workshops. (www.fabrianoboutique.com; Via del Corso 59r; ⊙10am-7.30pm Mon-Sat, 11am-7pm Sun)

A Piedi Nudi nel Parco FASHION

33 Map p36, E4

Specialising in high-end avant-garde designers, this place is so chic it even

has a tiny bar serving *aperitivi* (from 6pm) while you shop. (www.pnp-firenze. com; Via del Proconsolo 1; ⊙10.30am-7.30pm)

Mercato Nuovo MARKET

34 Map p36, C5

Stalls spilling over with cheap leather goods fill this 16th-century loggia, called the 'new market' to differentiate it from the 'old market' that stood here from the 11th century. Don't miss **Il Porcellino**, a bronze statue of a wild boar – rub its shiny snout (the legend goes) to ensure your return to Florence. (Loggia Mercato Nuovo; ⊙8.30am-7pm Mon-Sat)

Explore

Santa Maria Novella

Anchored by its magnificent basilica, this ancient and intriguing part of Florence defies easy description – from the rough-cut streets around the station it's only a short walk to the busy social scene around recently gentrified Piazza di Santa Maria Novella and the hip boutiques on the atmosphere-laden 'back streets' west of Via de' Tornabuoni.

The Sights in a Day

☀ Enjoy one of Florence's finest cappuccinos at **Caffè Giacosa** (p58) amid the engaging, prework hub-bub of Florentines downing espresso shots. Then meander north to the monumental hulk of **Basilica di Santa Maria Novella** (p50). Spend the morning exploring the sacred complex and its repository of Renaissance frescoes.

☀ Lunch local at **Mariano** (p56), a tiny wine bar with tasty, made-to-measure *panini* (sandwiches). Eat in with a glass of wine or wander to the Arno for a picnic with **Ponte Vecchio** (p118) views – riverside or atop **Ponte Santa Trìnita** (p54). Afterwards, admire the brilliant frescoes inside oft-overlooked gem **Chiesa di Santa Trìnita** (p54).

☾ Give your credit card an after-noon workout in the flagship stores of Italian fashion houses to the west of Via de' Tornabuoni. Allow ample time for the irresistible, old-world streets around here: Via della Spada is a particular delight and has the added lure of the startling Cappella Rucellai inside the **Museo Marino Marini** (p54). Stroll west to **Officina Profumo-Farmaceutica di Santa Maria Novella** (p61) – perfect for take-home gifts – then hit **Sei Divino** (p56) for that all-essential *aperitivo* (pre-dinner drinks accompanied by cocktail snacks). Dine nearby at **L'Osteria di Giovanni** (p56).

◉ **Top Sight**

Basilica Santa Maria Novella (p50)

♥ **Best of Florence**

Shopping
Letizia Fiorini (p58)

Mio Concept (p59)

Officina Profumo-Farmaceutica di Santa Maria Novella (p61)

Dolce Forte (p59)

Grevi (p60)

Alessandro Gherardeschi (p61)

Alberto Cozzi (p61)

Loretta Caponi (p61)

Drinking
Sei Divino (p56)

Caffè Giacosa (p58)

Eating
Mariano (p56)

L'Osteria di Giovanni (p56)

Getting There

From Piazza della Stazione Turn south into Via degli Avelli and you will almost immediately come to Piazza di Santa Maria Novella and its magnificent basilica.

Top Sights
Basilica di Santa Maria Novella

This monastery complex, fronted by the striking marble facade of its basilica, hides romantic church cloisters and a stunning frescoed chapel behind its monumental walls. The basilica – adorned with a luminous painted Crucifix by Giotto (c 1290) – is a Florence gem. Upon entering, head straight ahead to find Masaccio's superb fresco *Trinity* (1424–25), one of the first Renaissance artworks to use the newly discovered techniques of perspective and proportion.

◉ Map p52, G2

www.chiesasantamaria novella.it

Piazza di Santa Maria Novella 18

adult/reduced €5/3

⊘ 9am-5.30pm Mon-Thu, 11am-5.30pm Fri, 9am-5pm Sat, 1-5pm Sun

Ceiling frescoes inside Basilica di Santa Maria Novella

Don't Miss

Cappella Maggiore

Look behind the main altar to find the basilica's highlight, a tiny chapel adorned in vibrant frescoes painted by Ghirlandaio between 1485 and 1490. Relating the lives of the Virgin Mary, the frescoes are notable for their depiction of Florentine life during the Renaissance. Spot portraits of Ghirlandaio's contemporaries and members of the Tornabuoni family (who commissioned the frescoes).

Cappella Strozzi di Mantova

To the far left of the altar, up a short flight of stairs, is this wonderful chapel covered in soul-stirring 14th-century frescoes by Niccolò di Tommaso and Nardo di Cione. The fine altarpiece (1354–57) here was painted by the latter's brother Andrea, better known as Andrea Orcagna.

Chiostro Verde

From the church, walk through a side door into the serenely beautiful Green Cloister (1332–62), part of the vast monastery occupied by Dominican friars who arrived in Florence in 1219 and settled in Santa Maria Novella two years later. The cloister is named after the green earth base used for the frescoes on three of its four walls.

Cappellone degli Spagnoli

A door off the cloister's northern side leads into this chapel, named in 1566 when it was given to the Spanish colony in Florence (*Spagnoli* means Spanish). Its extraordinary frescoes (c 1365–67) by Andrea di Bonaiuto depict the Resurrection, Ascension and Pentecost (vault); on the altar wall are scenes of the Via Dolorosa, Crucifixion and Descent into Limbo.

☑ Top Tips

▶ Allow at least two hours to take it all in.

▶ Enter via the basilica on Piazza di Santa Maria Novella or through the tourist office opposite the train station on Via de' Partzani.

▶ Amuse yourself in the Spanish Chapel with a game of 'Spot the Celebrity ' – find portraits of Cimabue, Giotto, Boccaccio, Petrarch and Dante in *The Militant and Triumphant Church* fresco.

▶ Watch for the reopening (post renovation) of Cappella degli Ubriachi and the refectory with its 1583 *Last Supper* by Alessandro Allori.

✕ Take a Break

▶ Nearby Officina Profumo-Farmaceutica di Santa Maria Novella (p61) has a bijou tearoom where you can sip tea from bone-china cups.

▶ End on a culinary high with top-notch Tuscan cuisine at L'Osteria di Giovanni (p56).

A

B

C

D

Canale Macinante

Viale Fratelli Rosselli

Porta al Prato

Via Fosso Macinante

1

Via Il Prato

⊙5
Parco delle Cascine

Via Montebello

2

Via Magenta

Via G. Garibaldi

Via Palestro

12 ✿
Corso Italia

Via Curtatone

Lungarno Amerigo Vespucci

3

Arno

Lungarno di Santa Rosa

Ponte Amerigo Vespucci

4

Via dell'Anconella

Via Lungo le Mura di Santa Rosa

Via L Bartolini

Via Sant'Onofrio

Via del Piaggione

Via Pisana

Piazza di Verzaia

5

Viale Lodovico Ariosto

Piazza dei Nerli

Piazza del Tiratoio

SAN FREDIANO

N⊙ 0 _____ 200 m
     0 _____ 0.1 miles

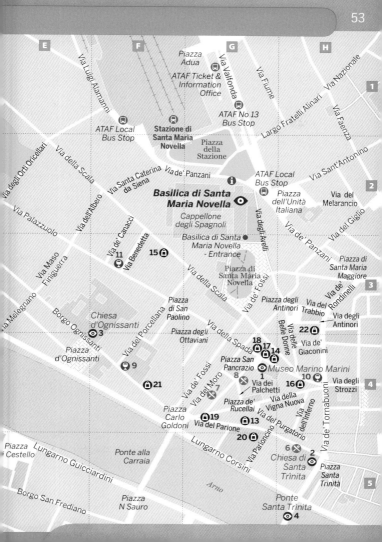

✓ Top Tip
Botticelli Essential

Having exhausted the master-pieces in the Uffizi Gallery, there is one more essential stop for Botticelli aficionados: the early Renaissance artist's grave inside **Chiesa d'Ognissanti**. The artist had requested to be buried at the feet of Simonetta Vespucci, the married woman whom Botticelli was said to be in love with and who served as a model for one of his greatest masterpieces, *Primavera* (Spring). Look for the simple round tombstone marked 'Sandro Filipepe' in the south transept. Botticelli grew up in a house on the same street and a pensive *St Augustine,* painted by him in 1480, hangs in the church.

Sights

Museo Marino Marini   ART GALLERY

1 ◉ Map p52, G4

The deconsecrated Chiesa di San Pancrazio hosts this small art museum displaying sculptures, portraits and drawings by the Pistoia-born sculptor Marino Marini (1901–80). But what really stuns is the superbly restored **Cappella Rucellai** and the tiny scale copy of Christ's Holy Sepulchre in Jerusalem – a Renaissance gem by Leon Battista Alberti – that it contains. (Piazza San Pancrazio 1; adult/reduced €4/2; ⊙10am-5pm Wed-Sat & Mon)

Chiesa di Santa Trìnita   CHURCH

2 ◉ Map p52, H5

Built in Gothic style and later given a Mannerist facade, this 14th-century church shelters fine frescoes including Lorenzo Monaco's *Annunciation* (1422) in the **Cappella Salimbenes/Bartholini** and frescoes (1483–85) by Ghirlandaio depicting the life of St Francis of Assisi in the **Cappella Sassetti,** to the right of the altar. The latter feature portraits of illustrious Florentines of the time. (Piazza Santa Trinita; ⊙8am-noon & 4-5.45pm Mon-Sat, 8-10.45am & 4-5.45pm Sun)

Chiesa d'Ognissanti   CHURCH

3 ◉ Map p52, F4

This 13th-century church, built as part of a Benedictine monastery, showcases Domenico Ghirlandaio's fresco of the *Madonna della Misericordia* protecting members of the Vespucci family, the church's main patrons. Amerigo Vespucci, the Florentine navigator who gave his name to the American continent, is supposed to be the young boy whose head peeks between the Madonna and the old man. (Borgo d'Ognissanti 42; ⊙7am-12.30pm & 4-8pm Mon-Sat, 4-8pm Sun)

Ponte Santa Trìnita   BRIDGE

4 ◉ Map p52, H5

Comprising three elliptical arches of the utmost elegance – the first of their kind ever used in bridge construction –

Ponte Santa Trinita

this bridge was designed in the 1560s by Ammannati, though its arches, reminiscent of the tombs in Cappelle Medicee, have led some to suspect Michelangelo's hand. Destroyed by Nazi bombs in 1944, it was reconstructed from the original stones retrieved from the Arno.

Parco delle Cascine   OUTDOORS

5 ⦿ Map p52, A1

When fresh air beckons, follow locals to Florence's largest city park for a frolick around fountains and across green lawns, a play in toddler-friendly playgrounds and a summertime splash in its open-air swimming pool. A hunting reserve for the Medici, Peter Leopold opened the park to the

public in 1776 – much to the delight of England's Queen Victoria, who frequented it during her sojourns in Florence. (Viale degli Olmi)

Local Life
Stazione di Santa Maria Novella

Most people rush through Florence's main station (Map p52, F1) without a second glance, but in fact it's one of Italy's great modernist buildings. Built in the early 1930s, the station's plain facade mimics the rough stone of churches such as San Lorenzo, while the red-and-white striped marble floors recall the city's official colours.

LONELY PLANET/GETTY IMAGES ©

Diners in Il Latini

L'Osteria di Giovanni

TUSCAN €€

7 🍴 Map p52, G4

It's not the decor that stands out at this friendly neighbourhood eatery. It's the cuisine, which is Tuscan and creative. Think chickpea soup with octopus, or pear and ricotta–stuffed *tortelli* (a type of ravioli) bathed in a leek and almond cream. Added extras include a complimentary glass of *prosecco* (a type of sparkling wine) and plate of *coccoli* (traditional Florentine salted fritters) as a starter. (📞055 28 48 97; www.osteriadigiovanni.it; Via del Moro 22; meals €35; 🕙dinner Mon-Fri, lunch & dinner Sat & Sun)

Il Latini

TRATTORIA €€

8 🍴 Map p52, G4

A veteran guidebook favourite built around melt-in-your-mouth *crostini* (toasts with various toppings), pasta and roasted meats served at shared tables. There are two dinner seatings (7.30pm and 9pm), with service ranging from charming to not so charming. Bookings mandatory. (📞055 21 09 16; www.illatini.com; Via dei Palchetti 6r; meals €35; 🕙lunch & dinner Tue-Sun)

Eating

Mariano

SANDWICHES €

6 🍴 Map p52, H5

Around since 1973 and our favourite for its simplicity. Sunrise to sunset, this brick-vaulted, 13th-century cellar gently buzzes with Florentines propped at the counter sipping coffee or wine. Come here for a coffee-and-pastry breakfast, light lunch (the salads are good), *aperitivo* or *panino* to eat on the run. (Via del Parione 19r; 🕙8am-3pm & 5-7.30pm Mon-Fri, 8am-3pm Sat)

Drinking

Sei Divino

WINE BAR

9 🍷 Map p52, F4

This stylish wine bar tucked beneath a red-brick vaulted ceiling is privy

Understand

The Renaissance

Though its streets and buildings date predominantly to the Middle Ages, it is the historical period known as the Renaissance (*Rinascimento*, or Rebirth) that defines Florence and remains its greatest moment.

In the second half of the 14th century, the city's power-brokers were keen to put the horrors of the plague of 1348, when more than 50% of the city's residents had perished, behind them. This catastrophic event had dealt a huge blow to their faith in God – what was truly powerful, they reasoned, was the intellect, resilience and beauty of human beings. The Renaissance preoccupation with Humanism was born.

An early and passionate convert to this way of thinking was Cosimo de' Medici (1389–1464), who used his massive fortune to fund a program of inspired cultural patronage. Painters, sculptors and architects were lured to Florence by the financial incentives and artistic opportunities he offered. Often inspired by the culture of classical antiquity, their works were as likely to celebrate the human body (eg, Michelangelo's *David*) or a pagan myth (Botticelli's *Birth of Venus*) as they were to re-work a standard religious theme. In architecture, the classical inspiration was even more pronounced, with Brunelleschi's design for the cathedral's massive dome forming the gold standard.

Alongside these developments in art and architecture was the flowering of Italian literature. Dante Alghieri's *La grande commedia* (The Great Comedy, later renamed the Divine Comedy) had been published around 1317 and established the Tuscan dialect as the new standardised form of written Italian. Giovanni Boccaccio (1303–75) and Francesco Petrarch (1304–74) were quick adaptors.

In the 15th and 16th centuries, developments in art, architecture and literature were matched by those in philosophy, political science and science, and Florence became home to a formidable intellectual milieu. This included artist, architect, scientist, engineer and all-round 'Renaissance man', Leonardo da Vinci (1452–1519); and writer, historian and political scientist, Niccolò Machiavelli (1469–1527).

As the 16th century drew to a close, so too did the Italian Renaissance. Fortunately, its heritage lives on and is showcased in the city's cultural institutions and deep appreciation (some would say obsession) with all things artistic.

Top Tip

Romance on a Budget

Before sunset, follow the lead of savvy, budget-conscious Florentines: buy a bottle of wine or your drink of choice, and head to the hottest seats in town – the smooth, stone platform created by the east-facing stone bridge supports of **Ponte Santa Trìnita**. Here, you can sit above the swirling water, drink al fresco and watch as the sun sinks behind the romantic, star-lit Ponte Vecchio further down the river.

to one of Florence's most happening *aperitivo* scenes. From the pale aqua-coloured Vespa parked up inside to the music, occasional exhibition and summertime pavement action, Sei Divino is a vintage that is eternally good. *Aperitivo* 'hour' kicks in from 5pm to 10pm. (Borgo Ognissanti 42r; ⏰10am-2am)

Caffè Giacosa   CAFE

10 Map p52, H4

This chic hangout is as famous for what it was – birthplace of the Negroni cocktail (1815) and a hub of Anglo-Florentine sophistication during the interwar years – as what it is (hip cafe of Florentine designer Roberto Cavalli, whose flagship store is next door). If you don't fancy the traffic-busy terrace here, head to its branch in nearby Palazzo Strozzi.

(www.caffegiacosa.it; Via della Spada 10r; ⏰7.45am-8.30pm Mon-Fri, 8.30am-8.30pm Sat, 12.30-8pm Sun)

Space Club   NIGHTCLUB

11 🎧 Map p52, F3

Sheer size alone impresses here – the moment you walk in, you'll know you are in for a good night of dancing, drinking and video-karaoke alongside a mixed student-international crowd. Put drinks on an electronic card 'tab' and pay at the end of the night (but risk forking out €50 if you lose the card). (www.spaceclubfirenze.com; Via Palazzuolo 37r; admission incl one drink €16; ⏰10pm-4am)

Entertainment

Teatro del Maggio Musicale Fiorentino   OPERA, BALLET

12 ⭐ Map p52, B2

The curtain rises on opera, classical concerts and ballet at this lovely theatre, host to the summertime festival Maggio Musicale Fiorentina. (📞055 28 72 22; www.maggiofiorentino.com; Corso Italia 16)

Shopping

Letizia Fiorini   PUPPETS

13 🔒 Map p52, G4

This charming shop is a one-woman affair – Letizia Fiorini sits at the counter and makes her distinctive puppets by hand in between assisting customers. You'll find Pulchinella (Punch), Arlecchino the clown, beautiful servant girl Colombina, Doctor Peste (complete with plague mask), cheeky Brighella, swashbuckling Il Capitano and many other characters from traditional Italian puppetry. (Via del Parione 60r; ☉10am-7pm Tue-Sat)

Mio Concept
HOMEWARES

14 🔒 Map p52, G4

A stunning and fascinating range of design objects for the home – some recycled or upcycled – as well as jewellery, T-shirts and so on, cram this stylish boutique created by German-born globetrotter Antje. The street sign art works by Florence-based street artist CLET are a real highlight. (www.mio-concept.com; Via della Spada 34; ☉3-7pm Mon, 10am-1.30pm & 2.30-7pm Tue-Sat)

Dolce Forte
CHOCOLATE

15 🔒 Map p52, F3

Elena is the passion and knowledge behind this astonishing chocolate shop. Think black truffle–flavoured chocolate, an entire cherry, stone et al, soaked in grappa and wrapped in white chocolate or – for the ultimate taste sensation – *formaggio di fossa* (a cheese from central Italy) soaked in sweet wine and enrobed in dark chocolate. (www.dolceforte.it; Via della Scala 21; ☉10am-1pm & 3.30-7.45pm Wed-Sat & Mon)

Understand

Giorgio Vasari: Pro or Con?

Giorgio Vasari (1511–74) takes flack from art historians: in a drive to 'purify' art, he painted over medieval frescoes in churches and public buildings, including the Basilica di Santa Maria Novella. He's even said to have painted over unfinished works by Leonardo da Vinci and Michelangelo in the Palazzo Vecchio to make way for his bombastic, floor-to-ceiling fresco cycle glorifying Duke Cosimo I.

Yet Vasari's pioneering series of biographies, *Le Vite delle più eccellenti pittori, scultori ed architettori* (Lives of the Most Excellent Painters, Sculptors and Architects) remain the basic text of Renaissance art studies.

As an architect, Vasari's most accommplished work was the elegant loggia of the Uffizi Gallery and the **Corridoio Vasariano**, an enclosed, elevated corridor running between the Uffizi and the Pitti Palace that is named in his honour.

Grevi

HATS

16 🔒 Map p52, H4

It was a hat made by Siena milliner Grevi that actress Cher wore in the film *Tea with Mussolini* (1999); ditto Maggie Smith in *My House in Umbria* (2003). So if you want to shop like a star, this hopelessly romantic boutique is the address. Hats range in price from €30 to unaffordable for many. (www.grevi.com; Via della Spada 11-13r; ⏰10am-2pm & 3-8pm Mon-Sat)

Aprosio & Co

ACCESSORIES, JEWELLERY

17 🔒 Map p52, G4

Ornella Aprosio fashions teeny, tiny glass and crystal beads into dazzling pieces of jewellery, hair accessories, animal-shaped brooches, handbags and even glass-flecked cashmere. It is all quite magical. (www.aprosio.it; Via della Spada 38; ⏰10.30am-1.30pm & 2.30-5.30pm Mon-Sat)

Desii Lab

FASHION

18 🔒 Map p52, G4

Be it a pair of glittering lilac and turquoise sequinned Uggs, patent

Officina Profumo-Farmaceutica di Santa Maria Novella

yellow Doc Martens or the latest Converse, this shoe and accessory shop – new and vintage – is the place to go. A street-fashion specialist, it has a couple of other fashion boutiques in town. (Via della Spada 40r; ⏰10am-7pm Mon-Sat)

Alessandro Gherardeschi

FASHION

19 🔒 Map p52, G4

Distinctive men's and women's shirts and blouses, short- and long-sleeved, in dozens of designs – floral, cupcakes, vintage cars, all sorts! – is what this colourful little designer boutique near the river sells. (Via della Vigna Nuova 97r; ⏰10am-7pm Mon-Sat)

Alberto Cozzi

STATIONERY

20 🔒 Map p52, G5

Florence is famous for its exquisite marbled paper and this well-known, fourth-generation bookbinder and restorer has been making sheets of the stuff by hand since 1908. Come here to buy paper, leather-bound journals and colourful cards. (Via del Parione 35r; ⏰10am-7pm)

Le Gare 24

FASHION

21 🔒 Map p52, F4

Waltz into this retro boutique near the river, note the bright turquoise sofa with hairy fuschia-pink cushions and know you're in one of the best

🔍 Local Life

Florence's Oldest Perfumery-Pharmacy

Florentines – and Italians generally – are huge fans of *erboristi* (shops selling botanical or herbal products), and **Officina Profumo-Farmaceutica di Santa Maria Novella** (Map p52, F3; www.smnovella.it; Via della Scala 16; ⏰9.30am-7.30pm), established way back in 1612, is without doubt the best-loved *erborista* in the city. The business took off when the Dominican friars of Santa Maria Novella began to concoct cures and sweet-smelling unguents using medicinal herbs cultivated in the monastery garden, and monks have been selling a range of fragrances, remedies, teas and skin-care products ever since.

addresses in town for cutting-edge fashion. (Borgo d'Ognissanti 24r; ⏰10am-8pm Mon-Sat)

Loretta Caponi

FASHION

22 🔒 Map p52, H3

An old family name dressing the aristocracy for eons, this utterly gorgeous shop sells hand-embroidered sleepwear, bed and table linen, as well as slippers, bathrobes and exquisitely smocked children's clothes. (www.lorettacaponi.com; Piazza degli Antinori 4r; ⏰10am-7pm Mon-Fri & Sat morning Mar-Oct, closed Mon afternoon Nov-Feb)

Explore

San Lorenzo & San Marco

This part of the city fuses a gutsy market precinct – covered produce market and noisy street stalls surrounding the Basilica di San Lorenzo – with capacious Piazza San Marco, home to Florence University and a much-loved museum. Between the two is the world's most famous sculpture, *David*. The result is a sensory experience jam-packed with urban grit and uplifting art.

The Sights in a Day

☼ Begin with a gulp of coffee and daily Florentine life inside the **Mercato Centrale** (p77). Exit on Via dell'Ariento and weave south along the chaotic alley of open-air stalls piled high with cheap clothes, leather and tourist kitsch emblazoned with *David*'s packet. Or dodge the clothes market – it can be overwhelming – by exiting on Piazza del Mercato Centrale and following Borgo la Noce to your next ports of call: **Basilica di San Lorenzo** (p66), **Biblioteca Laurenziana Medicea** (p71) and **Cappelle Medicee** (p70) (the latter two open mornings only).

☼ Medici opulence appreciated, quick-march into San Marco where the **Museo di San Marco** (p70) rewards with Fra' Angelico's haunting frescoes – the monastery museum closes at 1.50pm. Lunch late at **Antica Trattoria da Tito** (p73) or **Clubhouse** (p75).

☾ Spend a slower-paced afternoon in the **Galleria dell'Accademia** (p64), admiring the bewitching, concentrated expression of Michelangelo's *David,* highly charged in anticipation of the Goliath he is about to slay. Cool off afterwards with a gelato from **Carabé** (p76). Dine after dusk at **La Cucina del Garga** (p75).

👁 **Top Sights**

Galleria dell'Accademia (p64)

Basilica di San Lorenzo (p66)

♥ **Best of Florence**

Eating

Trattoria Mario (p73)

Antica Trattoria da Tito (p73)

Carabé (p76)

Art

Galleria dell'Accademia (p64)

Museo di San Marco (p70)

Cappelle Medicee (p70)

Palazzo Medici-Riccardi (p71)

Cenacolo di Sant'Apollonia (p73)

Getting There

From Piazza della Stazione Walk southeast along Via de' Panzani and turn left (northeast) into Via del Giglio, which takes you to the Cappelle Medicee, Piazza San Lorenzo and Basilica di San Lorenzo. Then walk east along Via de' Pucci and north into Via Ricasoli to reach the Galleria dell'Accademia and Piazza San Marco.

Top Sights
Galleria dell'Academia

A lengthy queue marks the door to this gallery, purpose-built to house one of the Renaissance's greatest masterpieces, Michelangelo's *David*. Fortunately, the world's most famous statue is worth the wait. The subtle detail of the real thing – the veins in his sinewy arms, the leg muscles, the change in expression as you move around the statue – is indeed impressive. Also here are Michelangelo's unfinished *Prigioni* sculpture and paintings by Andrea Orcagna, Taddeo Gaddi, Domenico Ghirlandaio, Filippino Lippi and Sandro Botticelli.

👁 Map p68, E3

www.polomuseale.
firenze.it

Via Ricasoli 60

adult/reduced
€6.50/3.25

🕐 8.15am-6.50pm
Tue-Sun

Michelangelo's *David*, Galleria dell'Academia

Don't Miss

Michelangelo's David

Carved from a single block of marble already worked on by two sculptors, Michelangelo's most famous work was challenging to complete. But when the statue of the nude boy-warrior – depicted for the first time as a man rather than young boy – appeared on Piazza della Signoria in 1504, Florentines immediately adopted *David* as an emblem of power, liberty and civic pride.

The Slaves

Another soul-soaring work by Michelangelo, *Prigioni* (1521–30) evokes four 'prisoners' or 'slaves' so powerfully that the figures really do seem to be writhing and struggling to free themselves from the ice-cold marble. The work was intended for the tomb of Pope Julius II in Rome, which was never completed.

Coronation of the Virgin

This remarkable piece of embroidery – an altar frontal 4m long and over 1m wide – portrays the *Coronazione della Vergine* (Coronation of the Virgin) in exquisite detail using polychrome silks and gold and silver thread. Completed by master embroiderer Jacopo Cambi in 1336, it originally covered the high altar of the Basilica di Santa Maria Novella.

Botticelli's Madonna

Madonna del Mare (Madonna of the Sea; 1477), a portrait of the Virgin and child by Sandro Botticelli, exudes a mesmerising serenity. Compare it with works in the gallery by Botticelli's master and mentor, Filippo Lippi (c 1457–1504), to whom some critics attribute it.

☑ Top Tips

▶ Prebook tickets at www.firenzemusei.it.

▶ Trail the world's best-known naked man around town: admire *David* copies on Piazza della Signoria and Piazzale Michelangelo, and see how other artists sculpted him in the Museo del Bargello.

✗ Take a Break

▶ Keep cool in the queue with a gelato or almond *granita* (ice drink) from Sicilian-style ice-cream shop, Carabé (p76).

▶ Grab a quick bite for lunch at La Forchetta Rotta (p73) or take your time over go-slow Tuscan at Antica Trattoria da Tito (p73).

Top Sights
Basilica di San Lorenzo

Founded in the 4th-century, San Lorenzo is considered Florence's oldest church. The current incarnation dates to 1425, when Cosimo the Elder hired Brunelleschi to spruce up the parish church to create a more suitable resting place for the Medici clan. The result: a gruff facade of rough-cut stones that belies an extraordinary, light-flooded interior. The harmonious internal arrangement of classical Corinthian columns of *pietra serena* (soft grey stone) was unlike anything seen before in Christendom.

👁 Map p68, C4

Piazza San Lorenzo

admission €4.50, with Biblioteca Medicea Laurenziana €7

🕙10am-5.30pm Mon-Sat, plus 1.30-5pm Sun Mar-Oct

Basilica di San Lorenzo

Don't Miss

Facade

The basilica is considered one of the most harmonious examples of Renaissance architecture, yet it was never finished. Medici pope Leo X commissioned Michelangelo to design the facade in 1518, but his design in white Carrara marble was never executed and the building has retained its rough and extremely unattractive underlayer ever since.

Sagrestia Vecchia

Left of the altar, opening off the north transept, lies the Old Sacristy, an important part of Brunelleschi's design. Decorated predominantly by Donatello, it features his painted *Tondo* and sculpted doors portraying martyrs and the apostles. Inside the domed space, designed as a cube (representing earth) topped by a sphere (symbolising heaven), lie several Medici tombs.

Donatello

Donatello, who sculpted the church's two bronze pulpits (1460–67) adorned with panels of the Crucifixion, is buried in the north-transept Chapel of the High Altar (also here is Fra' Filippo Lippi's c 1450 *Annunciation*). By Donatello's side rests Cosimo the Elder, the Medici who greatly admired and paid for much of the artist's work.

Mannerist Art

Two outstanding pieces of Mannerist art stand out: Rosso Fiorentino's *Sposalizio della Vergine* (Marriage of the Virgin Mary; 1523), with its handsome young Joseph; and Bronzino's gruesomely vivid fresco of the martyrdom of Saint Lawrence, the church's namesake.

☑ Top Tips

▶ Pretty cloisters framing a garden shaded with orange trees lie beyond the basilica ticket office – allow time to linger here in peace (and shade).

▶ Visit the basilica on a weekday morning when the Biblioteca Laurenziana Medicea (p71) and Cappelle Medicee (p70) are open (the Cappelle Medicee are closed some Mondays).

▶ Watch your pockets in the crowds that cram the San Lorenzo street market on the square in front of the basilica.

✕ Take a Break

▶ Push your way past market stalls to Trattoria Mario (p73) for a lunch to remember; arrive at noon or even earlier to snag a table.

▶ Go local: follow the lunchtime crowd to Da Nerbone (p75) for a steaming bowl of *trippa alla fiorentina* (tripe and tomato stew).

E

Duca d'Aosta
Via San Gallo ✕ 11
Via Cavour

F

Via Gustavo Modena
Via Venezia
Via Pier Antonio Micheli

G

Viale Giacomo Matteotti
Piazza Savonarola
Via G Benivieni
Via dei della Robbia
Via Pier Capponi

H

Piazza M Ficino
Piazza A Conti

1

Piazza I del Lungo
Via Gino Capponi

2

Via degli Artisti

Via Giorgio la Pira
Giardino dei Semplici

Giardino della Gherardesca

Piazzale Donatello

useo di
n Marco
1 ◉
Piazza
🚇 San Marco

Cimitero degli Inglesi

3

Via Cesare Battisti

Via Giuseppe Giusti

rd. Ricasoli
◉
Galleria
dell'Accademia

Piazza
della SS
Annunziata

Chiesa della
6 Santissima
◉ Annunziata

7 ◉ Museo
Archeologico

Via P Giordani

5 ◉
Ospedale
degli
Innocenti

Via Laura
Via della Colonna

Via dei Servi
21
🚻

Via del Castellaccio

Piazza
Brunelleschi

Via degli Alfani

Borgo Pinti

Piazza
Massimo
d'Azeglio

4

Via Vittorio Alfieri

Bufalini

23
🚻
Via Nuova de'
Caccini

Via Giosuè Carducci

22
🚻

18
✕

Via de' Pilastri

8 ◉
Synagogue
& Jewish
Museum of Florence

5

Piazza
di Santa
Maria Nuova

Via della Pergola

20
🚻

Via Luigi Carlo Farini

Borgo Pinti

Via de' Pepi

Via Sant'Egidio

17
✕

25
🔒

Via Fiesolana

Via di Mezzo

Via dell'Oriuolo

Sights

Museo di San Marco   MUSEUM

1  Map p68, E3

Comprising the **Chiesa di San Marco** and adjoining 15th-century Dominican **monastery**, this is Florence's most spiritually uplifting museum. It showcases the work of Fra' Angelico (c 1395–1455), a Tuscan friar and painter who decorated the cells with deeply devotional frescoes to guide the meditation of his fellow friars. His most famous work, *Annunciation* (c 1440), is found at the top of the stairs. (www.polomuseale.firenze.it; Piazza San Marco 1; adult/reduced €4/2; ⏰8.15am–

1.20pm Mon-Fri, to 4.20pm Sat & Sun, closed 1st, 3rd & 5th Sun & 2nd & 4th Mon of month)

Cappelle Medicee   MAUSOLEUM

2  Map p68, C4

The highlight of these sumptuous chapels, the final resting place of 49 Medicis, is the **Sagrestia Nuova** (New Sacristy) designed by Michelangelo. It showcases three of his most haunting sculptures: *Dawn and Dusk* on the sarcophagus of Lorenzo, Duke of Urbino; *Night and Day* on the sarcophagus of Lorenzo's son Giuliano; and *Madonna and Child* on Lorenzo's tomb. (Medici Chapels; ☎055 29 48 83; www.polomuseale.firenze. it; Piazza Madonna degli Aldobrandini; adult/

Chiesa della Santissima Annunziata (p72) and statue of Ferdinando I de' Medici

Understand
Who's that Bloke?

Name: David

Occupation: World's most famous sculpture

Vital statistics: 516cm tall, 19 tonnes of mediocre-quality, pearly-white marble from Carrara

Previous residences: Commissioned in 1501 for the Duomo, but subsequently placed in front of Palazzo Vecchio on Piazza della Signoria, where he stayed until 1873.

Favourite journeys: It took 40 men four days to transport the statue along rails from Michelangelo's workshop behind the Duomo to Piazza della Signoria in 1504. Its journey to the Galleria dell'Accademia in 1873 took seven days.

Why the small dick?: In classical art a large packet was not deemed elegant.

And the big head and hands?: *David* was designed to stand up high on a cathedral buttress in the apse, from which his head and hand would have appeared in proportion.

Occupational hazards: Over the centuries he's been struck by lightning and attacked by rioters. The two lines visible on his lower left arm are the spot where his arm was broken during the 1527 revolt when the Medicis were kicked out of Florence.

reduced €6/3; ⊙8.15am-1.20pm, closed 2nd & 4th Sun & 1st, 3rd & 5th Mon of month)

Biblioteca Medicea Laurenziana   LIBRARY

3 ⊙ Map p68, C4

Accessed via a door to the left of the Basilica di San Lorenzo's facade is the cloister, from which stairs lead to the loggia and this library commissioned by Giulio de' Medici (Pope Clement VII) in 1524. The staircase in the vestibule, intended as a 'dark prelude' to the magnificent **Sala di Lettura** (Reading Room), was designed by

Michelangelo. (Medici Library; www.bml.firenze.sbn.it; Piazza San Lorenzo 9; admission €3, incl basilica €7; ⊙9.30am-1.30pm Mon-Fri)

Palazzo Medici-Riccardi   PALACE

4 ⊙ Map p68, D4

The Medicis lived in this 15th-century *palazzo* (palace) until 1540, selling it to the Riccardi family a century later. It hosts excellent temporary exhibitions, but the major drawcard is a series of wonderfully detailed frescoes (c 1459–63) by Benozzo Gozzoli in the bijou **Cappella dei Magi**.

Local Life
Secret Garden

Founded in 1545 by the Medicis, the **Giardino dei Semplici** (Orto Botanico di Firenze, Florence Botanical Garden; Map p68, F3; ☏055 275 74 02; www.unifi.it/msn; Via Pier Antonio Micheli 3; adult/child €4/2; ☺9am-1pm Mon, Tue, Thu & Fri, to 5pm Sat) — today tended by the Università degli Studi di Firenze (University of Florence) — makes a welcome retreat in a stretch of the city with very little green space. Medicinal plants, Tuscan spices, and wildflowers from the Apennines fill the garden's 2.3 hectares and fragrant citrus-blossoms fill its greenhouse.

Only 10 visitors can visit the chapel at a time; reserve at the ticket desk or by telephone. (☏055 276 03 40; www.palazzo-medici.it; Via Cavour 3; adult/reduced €7/4; ☺9am-6.30pm Thu-Tue summer, to 5.30pm winter)

Ospedale degli Innocenti
GALLERY

5 ◉ Map p68, F3

Brunelleschi designed the portico for Europe's first orphanage in 1421, shortly after its founding, and Andrea della Robbia (1435–1525) added the charming terracotta medallions of swaddled babies. The false door surrounded by railings at the north end was once a revolving door where unwanted children were left.

(Hospital of the Innocents; Piazza della SS Annunziata 12)

Chiesa della Santissima Annunziata
CHURCH

6 ◉ Map p68, F3

Established on majestic Piazza della Santissima Annunziata in 1250 by the founders of the Servite order and rebuilt by Michelozzo in the mid-15th century, this Renaissance church is remarkable for its frescoes by the post-Renaissance painters who founded the Mannerist school: Andrea del Castagno, del Sarto, Jacopo Pontormo and Il Rosso Fiorentino (the Redhead from Florence). (Piazza Santissima Annunziata)

Museo Archeologico
MUSEUM

7 ◉ Map p68, F3

When the city's signature Renaissance splendor simply gets too much, retreat to Florence's small archeological museum. Its rich collection of finds – including most of the Medici hoard of antiquities – includes collections of ancient Egypt, Etruscan and Graeco-Roman art. (Piazza Santissima Annunziata 9b; adult/reduced €4/2; ☺8.30am-7pm Tue-Fri, to 2pm Sat-Mon)

Synagogue & Jewish Museum of Florence
SYNAGOGUE

8 ◉ Map p68, G5

Built in the 1870s just after the Jewish community in Italy had gained full emancipation after centuries of persecution, this vast synagogue is a beautiful, polychrome hodgepodge of Islamic, Jewish and Christian religious architecture. A small museum documents the history of Jewish Florence. (Sinagoga e Museo Ebraico di Firenz; ☎055 234 66 54; www.coopculture.it; Via Farini 6; admission adult/reduced/child under 6 €6.50/5/free; ☉10am-5.45pm Sun-Thu & to 4.15pm Fri Jun-Sep, 10am-4.45pm Sun-Thu & to 2.15pm Fri Oct-May)

Cenacolo di Sant'Apollonia
CONVENT

9 ◉ Map p68, D2

Once part of a sprawling Benedictine monastery, this *cenacolo* (frescoed refectory) harbours arguably the city's most remarkable Last Supper scene. Painted by Andrea del Castagno in the 1440s, it is one of the first works of its kind to effectively apply Renaissance perspective and has a haunting power. (☎055 238 86 07; Via XXVII Aprile 1; ☉8.15am-1.50pm Tue-Sat, 1st, 3rd & 5th Mon, 2nd & 4th Sun)

Eating

Trattoria Mario
TUSCAN €

10 ✖ Map p68, C3

Arrive by noon to ensure a stool at a shared table at this noisy, busy, brilliant trattoria – which retains its allure with locals despite being in every guidebook. Charming Fabio, whose grandfather opened it in 1953, is front of house while big brother Romeo and nephew Francesco are in the kitchen. No advance reservations; no credit cards. (www

.trattoriamario.com; Via Rosina 2; meals €20; ☉noon-3.30pm Mon-Sat, closed 3 wks Aug; ❋)

Antica Trattoria da Tito
TRATTORIA €€

11 ✖ Map p68, E1

The 'No well-done meat here' sign strung in the window says it all: the best of Tuscan culinary tradition is the only thing this iconic trattoria serves. In business since 1913, it does everything right – tasty dishes including onion soup and wild-boar pasta, served with gusto and hearty goodwill to a local crowd. Don't be shy to enter. (☎055 47 24 75; www.trattoriadatito.it; Via San Gallo 112r; meals €30; ☉lunch & dinner Mon-Sat)

La Forchetta Rotta
TUSCAN €

12 ✖ Map p68, D1

Run by the dynamic duo behind Santa Croce's Monkey Bar (p88), this place is staggeringly good value and tasty

☑ Top Tip

Fish Friday, Beef Saturday

In the finest of Tuscan dining tradition, many a trattoria address in Florence cooks up a different traditional dish each day of the week. For the folks at Trattoria Mario (left), Monday and Thursday are tripe days, Friday is fish and Saturday sees local Florentines flock in for a brilliantly blue *bistecca alla fiorentina* (T-bone steak; €35 per kilo).

Understand

The Medicis

Nowhere is a family name as linked with a city's identity as in Florence.

Harking from the Mugello region north of Florence, the Medicis were involved in the wool trade in the 13th and early 14th century. Though successful, they only came to prominence during the late 14th century, when Giovanni di Bicci de' Medici (1360–1429) established the Medici Bank. By the 15th century it was the largest in Europe. Giovanni's son Cosimo ('The Elder'; 1389–1464) used the vast family fortune to control local politics, becoming *gran maestro* (unofficial head of state) of the Florentine republic in 1434. A humanist, he was an enlightened patron of Florentine culture and arts.

Cosimo's son Piero (1416–69) succeeded his father as *gran maestro* but didn't have his penchant for patronage or skill in politics. His son and heir Lorenzo ('The Magnificent'; 1449–92) fully embraced his grandfather's interest in politics and culture, but had no interest in the bank. After his death it became apparent that the bank was in financial trouble, a situation exacerbated by his incompetent son and heir Piero (1472–1503). Piero's short reign as *gran maestro* culminated in the dynasty's exile from Florence in 1494.

Lorenzo's reputation and wealth had ensured that his second son, Giovanni di Lorenzo de' Medici (1475–1521), attained a powerful position in the Church; he became pope in 1513 (as Leo X). His cousin Giulio de' Medici (1478–1535) followed in his footsteps, being elected pope in 1523 and taking the name Clement VII. Both continued the Medici tradition of arts patronage.

The Medicis returned to Florence in 1512, but few were as talented or successful as their forebears. The most impressive was Cosimo I (1519–74), an ambitious soldier who became Duke of Florence and then the first Grand Duke of Tuscany. He was also a great patron of the arts.

After the Medicis' defeat by the House of Lorraine, Anna Maria Luisa de' Medici (1667–1743) willed the family's assets (including its magnificent art collection) to the Tuscan state, provided that nothing was ever removed from Florence.

to boot. At lunch, its kitchen caters predominantly to local workers and the result is superb: your pick of three or four homespun *primi* (first course), *secondi* (second course) and *contorni* (side dishes) for €7.50. The *aperitivo* (pre-dinner drinks accompanied by cocktail snacks) banquet laid out from 7pm onwards is equally generous. (☎055 384 19 98; Via San Zanobi 126r; lunch/dinner €7.50/25; ☺lunch & dinner Mon-Sat)

La Cucina del Garga   TUSCAN €€

13 🍴 Map p68, C2

La Cucina is a contemporary reincarnation of the original Garga, the San Frediano trattoria that wooed Florentine tastebuds for more than three decades. Run by Alessandro Gargani, New York chef and son of Giuliano 'Garga' Gargani, it features boldly painted walls crammed with modern art, another Garga trademark. Reservations are essential at weekends. (☎055 47 52 86; www.garga.it; Via San Zanobi 33r; meals €30)

Da Nerbone   MARKET STALL €

14 🍴 Map p68, C3

Forge your way past cheese, meat and sausage stalls in Florence's Mercato Centrale to join the lunchtime queue at Nerbone, in the biz since 1872. Go local and order *trippa alla fiorentina* (tripe and tomato stew) or follow the crowd with a feisty *panino con bollito* (a hefty boiled-beef bun, dunked in the meat's juices before serving).

RICHARD I'ANSON/GETTY IMAGES ©

Mercato Centrale (p77)

(Mercato Centrale, Piazza del Mercato Centrale; ☺7am-2pm Mon-Sat)

Clubhouse   AMERICAN, PIZZERIA €

15 🍴 Map p68, D4

This cavernous American bar, pizzeria and restaurant is close to the Galleria dell'Accademia and makes for the perfect dining-drinking hybrid any time of day (including Sunday brunch). Design buffs will appreciate its faintly industrial vibe and foodies will love its pizza-making courses. Gluten-free menu and €7 cocktail *aperitivi* from 6pm. (☎055 21 14 27; www.theclubhouse.it; Via de' Ginori 6r; pizza €6-12, meals €20; ☺noon-midnight)

Carabé
GELATO €

16   Map p68, D4

The almond *granita* at the Sicilian-style Carabé gelateria gets our vote for the most refreshing concoction on the planet. Produced with sizzling passion by Antonio and Loredana Lisciandro, the shop's gelati and *sorbetti* (sorbets) are top quality, perhaps best enjoyed in the form of a *brioche* (a Sicilian ice-cream sandwich). (www.gelatocarabe.com; Via Ricasoli 60r; ⊙10am-midnight, closed mid-Dec–mid-Jan)

Oil Shoppe
SANDWICHES €

17   Map p68, F5

Queue at the back of the shop for hot *panini* (sandwiches) and at the front

for cold at this busy student favourite. Pick from 29 different choices, climaxing with chef Alberto Scorzon's 10-filling wonder. (Via Sant'Egidio 22r; panini €3-4.50; ⊙11am-5pm Mon-Fri)

Acquacotta
TRATTORIA €

18   Map p68, G5

With its red-and-white checked tablecloths, terracotta tile floor and lace curtains, Acquacotta is everything a traditional Florentine eatery should be. Cuisine is as traditional as decor and the €12.50 lunch deal – two courses plus water and wine – is a steal. Advance reservations essential for dinner. (☎055 24 29 07; Via dei Pilastri 51r; meals €25; ⊙lunch & dinner Tue-Sun)

Rex Caffè

Drinking

Kitsch   BAR

19 🚇 Map p68, D2

Chandelier-lit Kitsch sits next to a 14th-century pilgrim hospice and lures 20- to early 30-something hipsters out for a good time with its lovely shabby-chic exterior, animal-print seats, pavement terrace and lavish spread at *aperitivo* time – €8.50 for a drink and sufficient nibbles to not need dinner. DJ sets set the place rocking after dark. (www.kitschfirenze.com; Via San Gallo 22r; ⏰6.30pm-2.30am)

Rex Caffé   BAR

20 🚇 Map p68, F5

A veteran favourite, Rex continues to remain ahead of the nightlife curve. DJs spin electronica that generally remains soft enough for the trendy, young crowd to engage in conversation. The decor is classy kitsch, mixing cracked pottery mosaics (think Gaudí), low but warm lighting from wrought-iron fixtures and a back room done up in blood red. (Via Fiesolana 25r; ⏰6pm-3am Sep-May)

Entertainment

Be Bop Music Club   LIVE MUSIC

21 ⭐ Map p68, E4

Inspired by the swinging sixties, this beloved retro bar and live-music

---

Local Life
At the Market

No single address proffers such a warts 'n' all glimpse into local life as Florence's central market. Feisty, frenetic and generally jam-packed, the 19th-century iron-and-glass hangar of the **Mercato Centrale** (Map p68, C3; Central Market; Piazza del Mercato Centrale; ⏰7am-2pm Mon-Fri, to 5pm Sat) is the place to buy everything from tripe and *pulmone* (cow's lung) to award-winning Tuscan olive oils, parmesan wheels, seasonal fruit, veg and wild herbs.

---

venue features everything from Led Zeppelin and Beatles cover bands to swing jazz and 1970s funk. (Via dei Servi 76r; admission free; ⏰9pm-2am)

Jazz Club   JAZZ

22 ⭐ Map p68, F5

Florence's top jazz venue hosts quality acts, both local and from wider afield, in an atmospheric vaulted basement. Besides jazz, you can catch salsa, blues, Dixieland and world-music acts. (Via Nuovo de' Caccini 3; ⏰10pm-2am Tue-Sat, closed Jul & Aug)

Teatro della Pergola   THEATRE

23 ⭐ Map p68, F4

Built in the 1650s, this small but wonderful baroque theatre with a stunning entrance is the ideal venue

> Understand
>
> ## The Saint & the Sinner
> ------------------------------
>
> Few artists are saints – they're far more likely to be sinners. One of the great exceptions was Fra' Angelico (c 1395–1455), the Renaissance painter who was known for centuries as 'Il Beato Angelico' (literally 'The Blessed Angelic One') or simply 'Il Beato' (The Blessed). Also a Dominican friar, Il Beato was canonised by Pope John Paul II in 1982. The best place to admire Fra' Angelico's work is the Museo di San Marco.
>
> Filippo Lippi (1406–69), one of the greatest Tuscan painters of his era, entered the Carmelite order as a monk aged only 14 but renounced his vows after meeting (and subsequently eloping with) a novice who was sitting for the figure of the Madonna in a fresco he was painting for the *duomo* in Prato. Their son Filippino (1457–1504) inherited his father's artistic talent but history doesn't record if he shared his father's peccadillos. The best place to appreciate the work of both generations is the Uffizi Gallery.

for chamber music. It also stages classic plays, from Shakespeare to Pirandello. The season runs October to April. (055 2 26 41; www.teatrodella-pergola.com; Via della Pergola 18)

Shopping

Check out the City of Artisans local life feature (p114) for details on where to buy unique, hand-crafted goodies.

Scarpelli Mosaici   ART

24 Map p68, D4

The entire Scarpelli family works hard to preserve the art of *pietre dure*, puzzlelike marble mosaics, at this beautiful craft laboratory and art gallery in San Lorenzo. And if

master craftsmen Renzo and Leonardo Scarpelli have time, they just might give you a quick introduction to this beautiful yet incredibly painstaking Florentine craft dating back to the Renaissance. (055 21 25 87; www.scarpelli mosaici.it; Via Ricasoli 59r)

Mrs Macis   FASHION

25 Map p68, F5

Workshop and showroom of the talented Carla Macis, this eye-catching boutique – dollhouse-like in design – specialises in very feminine 1950s, '60s and '70s clothes and jewellery made from new and recycled fabrics. Every piece is unique and fabulous. (Borgo Pinti 38r; 4-7.30pm Mon, 10.30am-1pm & 4-7.30pm Tue-Sat)

Archivi Fotografici Alinari
PHOTOGRAPHY

26 🔒 Map p68, B4

The world's oldest photographic firm has, since its founding in 1852, amassed an archive of some 3.5 million photographs, ranging from daguerreotypes to digital images. Its archives are open to the public, and you can still follow Lucy Honeychurch's lead in *A Room with a View* and order prints of the original photographs. (📞 055 2 39 51; www.alinari.it; Largo Fratelli Alinari 15; ⏰ 9am-1pm, 2-6pm Mon-Fri, closed 2 weeks mid-Aug)

Mesticheria Colorificio Poli
ARTS & CRAFTS

27 🔒 Map p68, C3

Step back in time at this shop specialising in rare paints, much of it still made by hand and scooped from ancient glass jars. Still run by the founder's grandchildren, the shop attracts perfectionist decorators as well as professional and amateur ceramicists. (📞 055 21 65 06; Via Guelfa 49r; ⏰ 9am-1pm & 2.30-7.30pm Mon-Sat, closed 2 weeks mid-Aug)

La Botteghina
CERAMICS

28 🔒 Map p68, D3

This unassuming little shop resembles dozens of others, but closer inspection reveals some of the city's best ceramics. Specialising in wares from nearby towns Montelupo and Deruta, the store sells objects made entirely by hand, many of which sport particularly vivid golds and vermillions. Given the quality of the work, prices are quite reasonable. (📞 055 28 73 67; www.labotteghinadelceramista.it; Via Guelfa 5r)

Passamaneria Toscana
FURNISHINGS

29 🔒 Map p68, C4

Specialising in brocade textiles in classical Florentine style, this shop is heavily laden with tassels, table runners, bed covers, pillowcases and wall hangings. It may have a work-a-day air, but the fabrics are rich, opulent and top-notch. A must if you want to recreate that Medici look back home! (📞 055 21 46 70; www.passamaneriatoscana.com; Piazza San Lorenzo 12r)

Conti Stefano
OLIVE OIL

30 🔒 Map p68, C3

This permanent market stall inside the Mercato Centrale is one of the finest places in Florence to buy Tuscan olive oil. Ask to taste it first to savour the difference between Tuscany's many different bitter, spicy, green and yellow olive oils; don't hesitate to ask for help and advice. (www.tuscanyflavours.com; Mercato Centrale; ⏰ 7am-2pm Mon-Fri, to 5pm Sat)

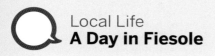

Local Life
A Day in Fiesole

Getting There

🚌 ATAF bus 7 (€1.20, 20 minutes, every 15 minutes) runs from Florence's Piazza San Marco to Fiesole's central square, Piazza Mino di Fiesole.

Set in cypress-studded hills 9km northeast of Florence, this bijou hilltop village has seduced visitors for centuries with its cool breezes, olive groves, Renaissance-styled villas and spectacular views. **Before you arrive, download the map from the website of Fiesole's tourist office** (📞 055 596 13 23, 055 596 13 11; www.fiesoleforyou.it; Via Portigiani 3, Fiesole; ⏰10am-6.30pm summer, shorter hr rest of yr). **It shows three walking routes through the village, as well as tips for discovering the most breathtaking views of Florence.**

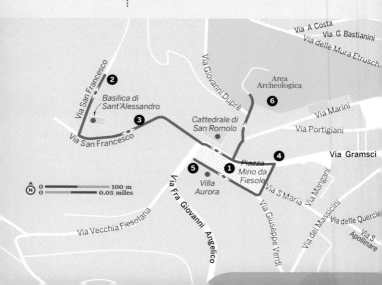

❶ People-Watch in the Piazza

Transport hub, *passeggiata* (evening stroll) hotspot and host to an antiques market on the first Sunday of each month, **Piazza Mino da Fiesole** is the heart of the village and a perfect choice for quality people watching. Claim a stone bench in the middle of the square or sit at a table at one of the restaurant terraces to view the action.

❷ A Contemplative Moment

The 11th-century Cattedrale di San Romolo, or *duomo* (cathedral), may be Fiesole's main religious monument, but it's not necessarily the best loved. The 14th-century **Chiesa di San Francesco** (🕑9am-noon & 3-6pm) is where locals come to snatch a contemplative moment or two during the day, stopping on their way here to admire the staggeringly beautiful panorama of Florence that unfolds from the terrace adjoining the 15th-century **Basilica di Sant'Alessandro**.

❸ Lunch at La Reggia degli Etrusch

Swoonworthy views and delicious Tuscan cuisine can be enjoyed on the panoramic terrace of this **restaurant** (📞055 5 93 85; www.lareggiadeglietruschi. com; Via San Francesco; meals €30; 🕑lunch & dinner daily) set in a former monastery close to the Chiesa di San Francesco. Florentines flock here on Sunday afternoons, but midweek lunches are still a mainly local affair.

❹ FiesoleBike

On weekends, cycling is a popular pastime. Join the local peloton by renting a bike from **FiesoleBike** (📞345-33 50 926; www.fiesolebike.it; Piazza Mino da Fiesole), operated by qualified biking and hiking guide, Giovanni Crescioli. GIovanni also conducts guided sunset cycling tours to Florence (downhill all the way!) and cross-country rides past farmhouses, churches, olive groves and vineyards.

❺ A Late-Afternoon Drink

For a reward after your exertions, head back to Piazza Mino da Fiesole where you can opt for local hangout **JJ Hill** (📞055 5 93 24; Piazza Mino da Fiesole 40; 🕑6pm-midnight Mon-Wed, 5pm-1am Thu-Sat, to 11pm Sun), an atmospheric Irish pub with a tip-top beer list, excellent burgers and other quality pub grub, or for the elegant, pagoda-covered terrace of **Villa Aurora** (📞055 5 93 63; www.villaurora.net; Piazza Mino da Fiesole 39; meals €30), a favourite with Fiesole's villa owners since 1860.

❻ Music Under the Stars

On summer nights, locals join urbane Florentines and the occasional bedazzled tourist in the 1st-century-BC Roman amphitheatre at Fiesole's Area Archeologica, off Piazza Mino da Fiesole, to enjoy the films, theatrical performances and musical concerts (jazz, classical and contemporary) staged as part of Italy's oldest open-air festival, **Estate Fiesolana** (www.estatefiesolana.it).

Explore

Santa Croce

Despite being only a hop, skip and jump from the city's major museums, this ancient part of Florence is far removed from the tourist maelstrom. The streets behind the basilica are home to plenty of locals, all of whom seem to be taking their neighbourhood's reinvention as hipster central – epicentre of the city's bar and club scene – with remarkable aplomb.

The Sights in a Day

☼ Start the day with a wander through the **Mercato di Sant'Ambrogio** (p92), pausing for a coffee at **Nano Caffè** (p89) before heading to the **Museo del Bargello** (p84) to admire its wonderful collection of Tuscan sculptures from the Renaissance period.

☼ Having made up your mind whose *David* you preferred (Michelangelo's or Donatello's?), head to bustling **Il Giova** (p92) for lunch; try to arrive close to noon so as to be sure of scoring a table. Afterwards, make your way to the neighbourhood's pride and joy, **Basilica di Santa Croce** (p86). When here, be sure not to miss the frescoed chapels in the main church and the exquisite Cappella de' Pazzi at the end of the first cloister.

☾ You're spoiled for choices when it comes to *aperitivo* (pre-dinner drinks accompanied by cocktail snacks) options – head to Via de' Benci and take your pick. Then lash out on a meal of a lifetime at **Enoteca Pinchiorri** (p93) or opt for a down-to-earth alternative at **Antico Noè** (p93). Finish the night bopping till you drop at **Blop Club** (p96).

For a local's night in Santa Croce, see p88.

👁 Top Sights

Museo del Bargello (p84)

Basilica di Santa Croce (p86)

◯ Local Life

A Night Out in Santa Croce (p88)

💜 Best of Florence

Eating

Il Giova (p92)

Enoteca Pinchiorri (p93)

Brac (p93)

Antico Noè (p93)

Francesco Vini (p94)

Pizzeria del' Osteria del Caffè Italiano (p95)

Vivoli (p93)

Drinking

Kitsch (p95)

Danny Rock (p95)

Lion's Fountain (p95)

Getting There

From Piazza della Stazione Walk southeast via Via de' Panzani, Via de' Cerretani and Via Proconsolo to Museo del Bargello. Take Via Ghibellina and turn right at Via Giuseppe Verdi south to Piazza di Santa Croce and its basilica.

Top Sights
Museo del Bargello

It was from the fortress-like Palazzo del Bargello – built in the mid-13th century and Florence's oldest still-standing public building – that the *podestà* (chief magistrate) meted out justice until 1502. Today the building safeguards Italy's most comprehensive collection of Tuscan Renaissance sculpture, including some of Michelangelo's best early works. While the crowds clamour to see his *David*, few rush to view his early works here – rendering the Bargello an art experience that is both contemplative and highly rewarding.

◉ Map p90, A2

www.polomuseale.firenze.it

Via del Proconsolo 4

adult/reduced €4/2, temporary exhibitions €6/3

🕙 8.15am-4.20pm Tue-Sun & 1st & 3rd Mon of month, to 2pm winter

David (bronze) by Donatello

Don't Miss

Michelangelo

Michelangelo was just 21 when he created the drunken, grape-adorned *Bacchus* (1496–97) displayed in the downstairs **Sala di Michelangelo**. Other Michelangelo works to look out for here include the marble bust of *Brutus* (c 1539–40), the *David/Apollo* (1530–32) and the large, uncompleted roundel of the *Madonna and Child with the Infant St John* (1503–05, aka the *Tondo Pitti*).

Sala di Donatello

The majestic salon where the city's general council met now showcases works by Donatello and other 15th-century sculptors. Don't miss his *St George* (1416–17), originally on the facade of Chiesa di Orsanmichele and now within a tabernacle at the hall's far end, which brought a new sense of perspective and movement to Italian sculpture.

Donatello's Davids

Donatello fashioned his slender, youthful dressed image in marble in 1408 and his fabled bronze between 1440 and 1450. The latter is extraordinary – the more so when you consider it was the first freestanding naked statue to be sculpted since classical times.

The Della Robbias

The 2nd floor features a superb collection of terracotta pieces by the prolific della Robbia family, including Andrea's *Ritratto idealizia di fanciullo* (Bust of a Boy; c 1475) and Giovanni's *Pietà* (1514). Instantly recognisable, Giovanni's works are more flamboyant than those of his father Luca or cousin Andrea, using a larger palette of colours.

☑ **Top Tips**

▶ Don't try to visit the Bargello and Uffizi together – their collections are too large and important to cram into a single day.

▶ Michelangelo devotees can follow a chronological trail of his sculptural works in Florence by visiting *David* at the Galleria dell'Accademia, stopping at the Cappelle Medicea to view the sculptures in the Sagrestia Nuova and then heading to the Bargello to admire his second *David* (aka *Apollo*) and the *Tondo Pitti*.

✖ **Take a Break**

▶ The most famous gelateria (ice-cream shop) in Florence, Vivoli (p93), is a only few blocks away.

▶ Head to artsy cafe-bookshop Brac (p93) for a coffee, *aperitivo* or vegetarian lunch.

Top Sights
Basilica di Santa Croce

The austere interior of this massive Franciscan basilica is a surprise when compared with its magnificent neo-Gothic facade, which is enlivened by varying shades of coloured marble. Though most visitors come to see the tombs of Michelangelo, Dante, Galileo and Machiavelli in the nave, it's the frescoes by Giotto and his school in the chapels to the right of the altar and the utterly exquisite Cappella de' Pazzi at the end of the first cloister that are the real highlights here.

👁 Map p90, B3

www.santacroceopera.it

Piazza di Santa Croce

adult/reduced €6/4, family ticket €12, combined ticket with Museo Casa Buonarroti €8.50

🕘 9.30am-5pm Mon-Sat, 2-5pm Sun

Basilica di Santa Croce

Don't Miss

Chapels

There are six frescoed chapels within the main church, with the most important being to the right of the main chapel and alter. The **Cappella Bardi** and **Cappella Peruzzi** were decorated by Giotto (1317–25), whose assistant and most loyal pupil, Taddeo Gaddi, worked on the **Cappella Baroncelli** (1328–38). Taddeo's son Agnolo frescoed the **Cappella Castellani** (c 1385).

Sagrestia

From the chapels, a doorway designed by Michelozzo leads into a corridor, off which you will find this enchanting 14th-century sacristy dominated on the left by Taddeo Gaddi's fresco of the Crucifixion. There are also a few relics belonging to St Francis on show, including his cowl and belt.

Museo dell'Opera di Santa Croce

Located off the first cloister, the basilica's museum features a Crucifixion by Cimabue, restored to the best degree possible after flood damage in 1966, when more than 4m of water inundated the Santa Croce area. Other highlights include Donatello's gilded bronze statue *St Louis of Toulouse* (1424), originally placed in a tabernacle on the Orsanmichele facade.

Cappella de' Pazzi

Brunelleschi designed this chapel at the end of the first cloister just before his death in 1446, and never saw it completed. It is notable for its harmonious proportions and its central dome, which is decorated with glazed terracottas by Luca della Robbia (look for two paired dolphins, the coat of arms of the Pazzi family).

☑ **Top Tips**

▶ Walk through the church bookshop to access the **Scuola del Cuoio** (p97), a leather school where you can see bags being fashioned and buy the finished products.

▶ In 1817, the French writer Stendhal experienced a racing heart beat, nausea and dizziness when exiting the basilica. His reaction to its cultural richness (and that of Florence as a whole) has been shared by many other visitors, hence the description 'Stendhal Syndrome'. Consider yourself warned!

✄ **Take a Break**

▶ Join the locals for lunch at Il Giova (p92), a bustling Tuscan trattoria.

▶ For an *aperitivo*, head to wine specialist Francesco Vini (p94). Sit inside amid the bottle-lined, red-brick walls or at an outdoor table in a hidden square.

Local Life
A Night Out in Santa Croce

In this heavily touristed city, it can be hard to find authentic pockets of local life. Fortunately, the fact that the basilica is the only top-drawer sight in Santa Croce means that the neighbourhood is blessedly bereft of sightseers – locals flock here to shop, eat, drink and party with their fellow Florentines as a result.

❶ Riverside Lounging
Begin what promises to be a great night out the Florentine way – soaking up the light, view and mood from a bridge across the Arno. Lounge with locals on **Ponte alle Grazie** as the sun softens and turns the river's romantic cascade of bridges a hazy mellow pink.

② Cocktails at Dusk

Nose-dive into trendy Via de' Benci with its bevy of bars and boutiques. Pop up to **Boutique Nadine** (www.boutiquenadine.com; Via de' Benci 32r; 2.30-7.30pm Mon, 10.30am-8pm Tue-Sat, noon-7pm Sun) to browse its vintage clothing and homewares before it closes. Then cross the street back to ever-popular **Moyo** (www.moyo.it; Via de' Benci 23r; 8am-2am Mon-Thu & Sun, 9am-3am Fri & Sat;) to enjoy a cranberry martini with lemon juice and triple sec (the house speciality).

③ Piazza di Santa Croce

Continue north along Via de' Benci to Santa Croce's central square. Cleared in the Middle Ages to accommodate an overspill of the faithful when its church was full, it now buzzes with buskers and street performers, kids playing football, locals lounging on benches in the soft evening sun and lovers rendezvousing by the statue of Dante.

④ Caffè Sant'Ambrogio

As the sun sets, stroll past artisan workshops to reach Piazza Sant'Ambrogio. Join locals for a drink in **Caffè Sant'Ambrogio** (www.caffesantambrogio.it; Piazza Sant'Ambrogio 7/r; 10.30am-3am Mon-Sat;), one of Santa Croce's original and iconic hangouts. Thirty-somethings still flock here for everything from morning espressos to lunch and late-night drinks.

⑤ Il Teatro del Sale

No Florentine chef is more charismatic than Fabio Picchi, whose eccentric **Il Teatro del Sale** (055 200 14 92; www.teatrodelsale.com; Via dei Macci 111r; breakfast/lunch/dinner €7/20/30; 9-11am, 12.30-2.15pm & 7-11pm Tue-Sat, closed Aug) occupies a fabulous old theatre and guarantees an unforgettable experience. Dinner is a hectic, mesmerising symphony of Tuscan dishes, culminating at 9.30pm in a live performance of drama, music or comedy arranged by Picchi's wife, comic actress Maria Cassi.

⑥ Late-Night Drinks

Show over, plunge into the star-lit night and follow the hip crowd to **Nano Caffè** (www.nanocaffe.info; Largo Annigoni, Piazza Ghiberti; 9am-3am), a design-driven L-shaped bar behind Sant'Ambrogio market that is much-loved by locals. Grab a seat under one of the large cream parasols on its al fresco terrace.

⑦ Monkey Bar

By midnight there's often a nip in the air. Time to duck behind Sant'Ambrogio market for a jar or shot at **Monkey Bar** (Via della Mattonaia 20r; 6pm-2am), a noisy pub that's always packed with a mix of Florentine and foreign students downing €2 shots, Spritz and well-made Bloody Marys. Italian double act Lorenzo and Freddy are the duo behind the place.

200 m
0.1 miles

Understand
Calcio Storico

It might well have been conceived to accommodate congregation overspill from the basilica, but it was inevitable that a space as vast and open as **Piazza di Santa Croce** would find other uses, too. Jousts and festivals have been staged here since the 14th century, as have matches of *calcio storico* (www.calciostoricofiorentino.it), a traditional sport that is a cross between football and rugby. This Florentine favourite pits 27 very burly men in brightly coloured costumes who beat each other bloody (literally) as they try to move the ball up and down the pitch. Sucker-punching and kicks to the head are forbidden, but few other rules apply – headbutting, punching, elbowing and choking are allowed. Games are played on the square each year during Florence's Festa di San Giovanni (June 24).

Look for the marble stone embedded in the wall below the gaily frescoed facade of Palazzo dell'Antella, on the south side of Piazza di Santa Croce; it marks the halfway line on what is essentially one of the oldest football pitches in the world.

Sights

Museo Casa Buonarroti

MUSEUM

1 ◉ Map p90, C2

Though Michelangelo never lived in Casa Buonarroti, his heirs devoted some of the artist's hard-earned wealth to the construction of this 17th-century *palazzo* (palace) to honour his memory. The little museum contains frescoes of the artist's life and two of his most important early works – the serene bas-relief *Madonna of the Stairs* (c 1491) and the unfinished *Battle of the Centaurs* (c 1492). (☏055 24 17 52; www.casabuonarroti.it; Via Ghibellina 70; adult/reduced €6.40/4.50; combined ticket with Basilica di Santa Croce €8.50; ☺10am-5pm Wed-Mon)

Museo Horne

MUSEUM

2 ◉ Map p90, A4

One of the many eccentric Brits who made Florence home in the early 20th century, Herbert Percy Horne bought and renovated this Renaissance *palazzo*, then installed his eclectic collection of 14th- and 15th-century Italian art, ceramics and other oddments. There are a few works by masters such as Giotto and Filippo Lippi, and some exquisite furniture. (☏055 24 46 61; www.museohorne.it; Via de' Benci 6; adult/child €6/4; ☺9am-1pm Mon-Sat)

Local Life
Mercato di Sant'Ambrogio

This **market** (Map p90, D2; Piazza Ghiberti; ⏱7am-2pm Mon-Sat) has a more local flavour than the larger and more high-profile Mercato Centrale in San Lorenzo. Food stalls dominate, and can be found in both the outdoor market and inside the produce hall (fruit and veg outside, meat and cheese inside). The best day to visit is Saturday, when farmers from the region travel here to sell produce straight from the field.

Eating

Il Giova   TRATTORIA €

3 ✗   Map p90, D1

Pocket-sized and perennially packed, this cheery trattoria is everything a traditional Florentine eating place should be. Dig into century-old dishes like *zuppa della nonna* (grandma's soup), *risotto del giorno* (risotto of the day) *or mafalde al ragù* (long-ribboned pasta with meat sauce) and pride yourself on finding a place to dine with locals. (☎055 248 06 39; www.ilgiova.com; Borgo La Croce 73r; meals €25; ⏱lunch & dinner Mon-Sat)

Bistecca alla fiorentina (T-bone steak), a local speciality

Enoteca Pinchiorri
GASTRONOMIC €€€

4 🍴 Map p90, B2

Chef Annie Féolde applies French techniques to her versions of refined Tuscan cuisine and does it so well that this is the only restaurant in Tuscany to brandish three Michelin stars. The setting is a 16th-century palace hotel and the wine list is mind-boggling in its extent and excellence. A once-in-a-lifetime experience. (☑055 24 27 77; www.enotecapinchiorri.com; Via Ghibellina 87r; 4-/8-course tasting menu €200/250; ⊙lunch & dinner Tue-Sat, closed Aug)

Brac
VEGETARIAN €

5 🍴 Map p90, A3

This hipster cafe-bookshop has a decor that relies on recycled vintage and a menu featuring inventive, home-style and strictly vegetarian and/or vegan cuisine. Reserve in advance at weekends and note that it can be tricky to find – there's no sign outside, just an inconspicuous doorway two streets back from the river with a jumble of books in the window. (☑055 094 48 77; www.libreriabrac.net; Via dei Vagellai 18r; meals €20; ⊙noon-midnight, closed 2 wks mid-Aug; 🌱)

Antico Noè
OSTERIA €

6 🍴 Map p90, B1

Don't be put off by the dank alley in which this old butcher's shop with white marble-clad walls and wrought-iron meat hooks is found. The drunks loitering outside are generally harmless and the down-to-earth Tuscan fodder served is a real joy. For a quick bite, opt for a *panino* (sandwich) from the adjoining *fiaschetteria* (small tavern). (Volta di San Piero 6r; meals €20; ⊙noon-midnight Mon-Sat)

Touch
MODERN TUSCAN €€

7 🍴 Map p90, C1

Hidden behind an elegant facade with frosted glass, this intimate dining space serves thoroughly contemporary dishes made with traditional Tuscan ingredients. Flip through the menu on an iPad (there's one on each table), look at images of each dish and enjoy

Local Life
A Gelato Break

Florentines take their gelato seriously and there's healthy rivalry among the operators of local gelaterie *artigianale* (shops selling handmade gelato), who strive to create the city's creamiest, most flavourful and freshest ice cream using seasonal flavours. In Santa Croce, **Vivoli** (Map p90, B2; Via dell'Isola delle Stinche 7; tub €2-10; ⊙7.30am-midnight Tue-Sat, 9am-midnight Sun summer, to 9pm winter) is the gelateria with the greatest number of devotees – try the pear and caramel flavour, or the chocolate with orange, and you'll find out why. Pay at the cash desk then trade your receipt for the good stuff. No cones, only tubs.

short videos showing how each is prepared before ordering – on the iPad, of course. (☎ 055 246 61 50; www.touchflorence.com; Via Fiesolana 18r; meals €40)

Trattoria Cibrèo

TRATTORIA €€

8 🍴 Map p90, D2

Dine here and you'll instantly understand why a queue inevitably gathers outside before it opens. Once in, revel in top-notch Tuscan cuisine. No advance reservations, no credit cards, no coffee and you'll need to arrive early to snag a table. (www.edizioniteatrodelsalecibreofirenze.it; Via dei Macci 122r; meals €30; ⊙lunch & dinner Tue-Sat, closed Aug)

Francesco Vini

TUSCAN €€

9 🍴 Map p90, A3

Built on top of Roman ruins, this wine specialist has two entrances – one with pavement terrace on people-busy Borgo de' Greci and a second, lovelier one on a hidden, quintessentially Florentine square. Winter dining is in a bottle-lined space. The wine list, jam-packed with Tuscan greats, is sensational. (☎ 055 21 87 37; www.francescovini.com; Piazza de' Peruzzi 8r, Borgo de' Greci 7r; meals €40; ⊙9am-midnight Mon-Sat)

Osteria del Caffè Italiano

TUSCAN €€€

10 🍴 Map p90, B2

Set in 14th-century Palazzo Salviati, this dining veteran serves classics such as ravioli stuffed with ricotta and *cavolo nero* (black cabbage), as well as the city's famous *bistecca alla fiorentina* (per kilo €60). Profiteroles and hot chocolate sauce provide a devilish finale. (☎ 055 28 93 68; www.osteriacaffeitaliano.com; Via dell'Isola delle Stinche 11-13r; meals €45; ⊙lunch & dinner Tue-Sun)

Drinking

Drogheria

LOUNGE BAR

11 🍷 Map p90, D2

Be it rain, hail or shine, this is a true Santa Croce favourite. Inside is a large vintage-chic space with soft, leaf-green chairs in which customers lounge for hours on end. Come spring, the action moves outside onto the terrace behind Sant'Ambrogio market. The kitchen cooks up bar-style dishes including burgers – beef, veggie, tofu or falafel. (www.drogheriafirenze.it; Largo Annigoni 22; ⊙10am-3am)

Soul Kitchen

BAR

12 🍷 Map p90, B3

Keep an eye out for flyers advertising the DJ sets, live music and various hip happenings that occur at this trendy design bar footsteps from Piazza Santa Croce. It also serves lunch, afternoon coffee and *aperitivo*. (www.soulkitchenfirenze.it; Via de' Benci 34r; ⊙11am-3am)

Kitsch BAR

13 🚇 Map p90, E1

This American-styled bar in Santa Croce is known among cent-conscious Florentines for its lavish spread at *aperitivo* time – €8.50 for drink and sufficient nibbles to not need dinner. It sports a dark-red theatrical interior and a bright 20- to early 30–something crowd out for a good time. DJ sets ensure a happening vibe after dark. (www.kitschfirenze.com; Viale A Gramsci 5; ⊘6.30pm-2.30am; 🛜)

Danny Rock BAR

14 🚇 Map p90, B2

Around since 1980, Danny Rock was given a new lease of life in late 2012 when new management waltzed in and revamped the place. Artisanal beer from around the globe is its main draw these days, alongside a bright and breezy interior, food all day, and charismatic owner Cosimo Lavacchi behind the bar. (www.dannyrock.it; Via de' Pandolfini 13r; ⊘10-2am; 🚇A)

Caffè Cibrèo CAFE

15 🚇 Map p90, D2

Duck into this charming old-world cafe behind Mercato di Sant'Ambrogio for a coffee and *ciambella* (doughnut ring). There's seating indoors and outdoors. (☎055 234 58 53; Via Andrea del Verrocchio 5; ⊘8am-1am Tue-Sat Sep-Jul)

Local Life
Pre-Club Pizza

What better fuel for a night spent bar and club hopping than a pizza pulled hot from a wood-fired oven? Places serving Neapolitan-style thick-crust pies are particularly popular, and two Santa Croce joints do their southern brothers proud: **Il Pizzaiuolo** (Map p90, D1; ☎055 24 11 71; Via dei Macci 113r; pizzas €5-10, pastas €6.50-12; ⊘lunch & dinner Mon-Sat, closed Aug), just off Piazza Sant' Ambrogio, and **Pizzeria del' Osteria del Caffè Italiano** (Map p90, B2; www.osteriacaffeitaliano. com; Via dell'Isola delle Stinche 11-13r; pizza €8; ⊘7.30-11pm), close to Piazza di Santa Croce. Be prepared to queue at nights and weekends and note that the *osteria* (casual tavern) only accepts cash.

Lion's Fountain IRISH PUB

16 🚇 Map p90, B1

If you have the urge to hear more English than Italian, this is the place. On a pretty pedestrian square, Florence's busiest Irish pub buzzes in summer when the beer-loving crowd spills out the door. Live music. (www.thelionsfountain. com; Borgo degli Albizi 34r; ⊘10am-2am)

Eby's Bar LATIN BAR

17 🚇 Map p90, B1

A lively student crowd packs out this young, fun, colourful address with wooden-bench tucked outside in a covered alleyway. The menu is Mexican. (Via dell'Oriuolo 5r; ⏱10am-3am Mon-Sat)

Lochness Lounge   MUSIC BAR

18 🎙 Map p90, A3

Run by Dane-turned-native Trine West, this sassy, vintage-cool music 'n' cocktail venue has a definite Andy Warhol twist to its bold pillarbox-red interior. DJs play alternative sounds most nights; check the website for the

🔍 Local Life
Go to Jail!

Florence's red-brick, old city jail (1883–1985) is now one of the city's most exciting cultural spaces. There's no mistaking the sturdy doors leading to the old prison cells, many of which now open onto the likes of a bookshop, a wine bar and an art gallery.

The pièce de résistance is **Le Murate Caffè Letterario** (Map p90, E3; 📞 055 234 68 72; www.lemu rate.it; Piazza delle Murate Firenze; ⏱9-1am), a cafe-bar where Florence's literati meet over coffee, drinks and light meals. The cafe hosts everything from readings and interviews with authors – Florentine, Italian and international – to film screenings, debates, live music and art exhibitions. Its funky interior has vintage chairs and table tops built from recycled window frames. In summer everything spills onto the wonderful brick courtyard. Check upcoming events online.

week's line-up. (www.lochnessfirenze.com; Via de' Benci 19r; ⏱7pm-2am)

Blob Club   NIGHTCLUB

19 🎙 Map p90, A3

No surprise that Florence's trendiest club of the moment is in this hip part of town. Small and edgy, Blob lures an international crowd with its music theme nights – loads of '60s, hip hop, alternative rock, all sounds in fact. No entrance fee, but first-timers need to buy a membership card (€20). (Via Vinegia 21r; ⏱11pm-3am Mon-Wed, to 5am Thu-Sat)

Twice Club   NIGHTCLUB

20 🎙 Map p90, B2

There's no admission but you need to look good to get past the bouncers on the door here. Once in, Twice is a relaxed club with stylish decor – chandeliers, no less – and a cocktail-quaffing crowd. Music is mainstream dance. Happy hour is 9pm to 11pm; don't expect action on the dance floor until well past midnight. (www.twiceclub.com; Via Giuseppe Verdi 57r; ⏱9pm-4am)

Shopping

Vintage di Antonini Alessandra   FASHION

21 🔒 Map p90, B2

For real-McCoy haute-couture pieces – Chanel handbags, strappy 1970s Dior sandals – look no further than this stylish boutique off Via delle Seggiole.

GMF/FIRENZE/ALAMY ©

Scuola del Cuoio

(Piazza Piero Calamandrei; ⏰3.30-7.30pm
Mon, 10.30am-1.15pm & 3.30-7.30pm Tue-Sat)

Mercato dei Pulci ANTIQUES

22 🔒 Map p90, C2

While prices are much higher than
the name implies (*mercato dei pulci*
means flea market), this outdoor market is nevertheless still worth a gander
for patient pickers keen to bring home
a piece of Old Tuscany. (Piazza dei
Ciompi; ⏰10am-1pm, 4-7pm Mon-Sat)

Scuola del Cuoio CLOTHING

23 🔒 Map p90, B3

In a courtyard behind Santa Croce, this
store and workshop features a long corridor where craftspeople stand at their
stations fashioning their leathergoods
by hand. You can buy the high-quality
wares at prices somewhat more reasonable than at most shops, though don't
expect to find bargains. (☎055 24 45 33;
www.scuoladelcuoio.com; Via San Giuseppe 5r;
⏰10am-6pm)

Explore

Boboli & San Miniato al Monte

If you start to suffer museum overload (a common occurrence in this culturally resplendent city), you may decide that it's important to stretch your legs and see some sky. If so, the tier of palaces, villas and gardens ascending to the Basilica di San Miniato al Monte, one of the city's oldest and most beautiful churches, will fit the bill perfectly.

The Sights in a Day

☀ Devote the morning to exploring the galleries and garden of the monumental **Palazzo Pitti** (p100), home at various times to members of the powerful Medici, Lorraine and Savoy families. Be sure to pop into the nearby **Giardino Bardini** (p105), too.

☀ Enjoy a well-deserved rest over lunch at **Da Ruggero** (p109), a traditional Tuscan trattoria, or opt for a glass of wine and a snack at **Enoteca Fuori Porta** (p109) – its range of Tuscan and Piemontese reds is particularly impressive. Afterwards, walk through San Niccolò, indulge in a spot of retail therapy at **Alessandro Dari** (p111) and **Lorenzo Villoresi** (p111), and then head up Via del Monte alla Croce to visit one of the city's Romanesque gems, the **Basilica di San Miniato al Monte** (p108).

☾ Watch the sun set over the city from **Piazzale Michelangelo** (p105) and make your way to **Le Volpi e l'Uva** (p110) for a pre-dinner drink. From here, the perennially popular restaurants and lounge bars of the Oltrano are only a short walk away.

For a local's day in Boboli & San Miniato al Monte, see p104.

👁 **Top Sight**
Palazzo Pitti (p100)

🔍 **Local Life**
Gardens of Florence (p104)

♥ **Best of Florence**

Views
Piazzale Michelangelo (p105)
Giardino di Boboli (p104)
Giardino Bardini (p105)
Basilica di San Miniato al Monte (p108)
Open Bar (p110)

Eating
Da Ruggero (p109)
Enoteca Fuori Porta (p109)

Drinking
Le Volpi e l'Uva (p110)
James Joyce (p111)

Getting There

From Piazza della Stazione Walk southeast along Via de' Panzani and Via de' Cerretani to the *duomo* (cathedral). Head down Via Roma, cross Ponte Vecchio and continue south along Via Guicciardini to Palazzo Pitti.

🚌 **Bus** Bus 13 runs to Piazzale Michelangelo.

Top Sights
Palazzo Pitti

Wealthy banker Luca Pitti commissioned Brunelleschi to design this huge palace in 1457, but by the time it was completed the family fortunes were on the wane and they were forced to sell it to arch-rivals, the Medicis. It subsequently became home to the dukes of Lorraine and their successors. When Florence was made capital of the nascent Kingdom of Italy in 1865, the palace became a residence of the Savoys, who presented it to the state in 1919.

👁 Map p106, C2

www.polomuseale.firenze.it

Piazza dei Pitti

adult/EU 18-25/EU child & senior Ticket 3 €11.50/5.75/free

🕓 8.15am-6.05pm Tue-Sun

Galleria Palatina, Palazzo Pitti

Don't Miss

Museo degli Argenti

Our recent stroll around this ground-floor museum was notable for the fact that no *argenti* (silver) was on display. Go figure. Come instead to see the elaborately frescoed audience chambers, which host temporary exhibitions. These include the **Sala di Giovanni da San Giovanni**, which sports head-to-toe frescoes celebrating the life of Lorenzo the Magnificent – spot Michelangelo giving Lorenzo a statue.

Galleria d'Arte Moderna

By modern, the Pitti's powers-that-be mean 18th and 19th century (again, go figure). So forget about Marini, Mertz or Clemente – the collection of this 2nd-floor gallery is dominated by late-19th-century works by artists of the Florentine Macchiaioli school (the local equivalent of Impressionism), including Telemaco Signorini (1835–1901) and Giovanni Fattori (1825–1908).

Galleria del Costume

The costume gallery features an absolutely fascinating, if somewhat macabre, display of the semidecomposed burial clothes of Cosimo I, his wife Eleonora di Toledo and their son Don Garzia. Considering the fact that they were buried for centuries, Eleanora's gown and silk stockings are remarkably preserved, as are Cosimo's satin doublet and wool breeches and Garzia's doublet, beret and short cape.

Appartamenti Reali

Accessed through the Galleria Palatina, these rooms are presented as they were c 1880–91 when the palace was occupied by members of the House of Savoy. The style and division of tasks assigned to each space is reminiscent of

☑ Top Tips

▶ Ticketing for the palace complex and surrounding gardens is complicated: choose from Ticket 1 (Galleria Palatina, Appartamenti Reali and Galleria d'Arte Moderna); Ticket 2 (Galleria del Costume, Museo degli Argenti, Giardino di Boboli, Giardino Bardini and Museo delle Porcellane); and Ticket 3 (all sights; valid for three days). Buy these from the ticket office to the right of the palace entrance.

✕ Take a Break

▶ In summer, head to the Giardino Bardini (entrance included in Tickets 2 and 3) to enjoy a coffee, a tea, a *panino* (sandwich) or an ice cream in its **cafe**, which is set in a stone loggia overlooking the Florentine skyline.

▶ In winter, enjoy a classic Tuscan meal at family-run Da Ruggero (p109).

Spanish royal palaces, and all are heavily bedecked with drapes, silk and chandeliers.

Galleria Palatina

This gallery, the palace's main attraction, houses an extraordinary collection of 16th- to 18th-century art amassed by the Medici and Lorraine grand dukes. The original arrangement of paintings (squeezed in, often on top of each other) has been retained and can be visually overwhelming – go slow and focus on the works one by one.

Tondo Bartolini

The gallery's highlights are found in a series of reception chambers dating from the Napoleonic period and decorated in the Neoclassical style. In the **Sala di Prometeo** is Fra' Filippo Lippi's *Madonna and Child with Stories from the Life of St Anne* (aka the *Tondo Bartolini;* 1452–53), one of the artist's major works.

Madonna with Child and a Young Saint John the Baptist

Also in the **Sala di Prometeo** is this sombre painting (c 1490–95) by Botticelli. Its subject and execution stand in stark contrast to his earlier, often hedonistic, works – probably because it was painted after the death of Lorenzo the Magnificent, Botticelli's great patron, and during the ascendancy of the fire-and-brimstone preacher, Savonarola.

Madonna of the Window

Named for the cloth-covered window in its background, this charming work by Raphael was painted in 1513–14, towards the end of his glittering artistic career. The painting is exhibited in the Sala di Ulisse, once the bedroom of the Grand Dukes of Tuscany.

Sleeping Cupid

The gallery's sentimental favourite is undoubtedly Caravaggio's *Sleeping Cupid,* painted in 1608 in Malta, where the painter had fled after killing a man in a brawl and being exiled from Rome as a consequence. You'll find it in the Sala dell'Educazione di Giove.

A Feast of Raphaels

The handsome **Sala dell'Iliade** showcases the artist's *Portrait of a Woman* (aka *La Gravida;* c 1505–06) and the **Sala di Saturno** is home to *Madonna with Child and St John the Baptist* (aka *The Madonna of the Chair;* 1511). Raphael's *Lady with a Veil* (aka *La Velata;* c 1516) holds court in the **Sala di Giove**.

Portrait of a Man

The Venetian painter Titian (c 1490–1576) was a master of the portrait, and this painting of an unknown man (*Ritratto Virile;* c 1540–45) is one of his best. Also known as *Portrait of a Young Englishman,* the subject displays a particularly piercing gaze. It's one of a number of Titians in the **Sala di Apollo**.

Fresco, Palazzo Pitti

Giardino di Boboli

Laid out in the mid-16th century, the Boboli Garden is a prime example of formal Tuscan garden design, blessed with plenty of water features, grottoes, statues and hidden paths. Highlights include the walled Giardino del Cavaliere (Knights' Garden), sculpture-adorned Anfiteatro (Amphitheatre) and grand Isolotto (Ornamental Pool). There's also a great view from the terrace at the top of the garden.

Grotta del Buontalenti

Hundreds of seashells decorate the facade of this fanciful grotto designed by the sculptor Giambologna. To see Venere (Venus) rising from the waves and to inspect the grotto's other sculptures, take one of the daily guided tours (11am, 1pm and 3pm year-round, with one or two later tours between March and September). No extra ticket is necessary.

Local Life
Gardens of Florence

Florence can be a noisy place. Its streets and piazzas reverberate with a constant cacophony of sounds – tour guides bellowing at their bewildered charges, locals enjoying an animated chat on their *passeggiata* (early-evening stroll), honking vespas weaving in-between mapwielding sightseers – which is why the tranquil public gardens in or around this neighbourhood are so treasured.

❶ Giardino di Boboli

Purchase Ticket 2 or Ticket 3 at the Palazzo Pitti ticket office and head to the rear of the building, where this huge formal **garden** (Boboli Garden; Piazza Pitti; adult/reduced/child €7/3.50/free; ☉8.15am-7pm summer, shorter hr winter) waits to be explored. Wander its many paths, admire the Isoloto and decide whether or not the Grotta del Buontalenti is an artistic masterpiece (we tend to think not).

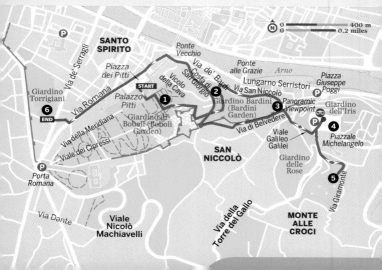

❷ Giardino Bardini

An impressive example of a formal Tuscan garden, the medieval **Giardino Bardini** (Bardini Garden; www.bardinipeyron.it; entrances at Via de' Bardi 1r & Costa di San Giorgio 2; adult/EU reduced €10/free, or with Palazzo Pitti Ticket 2 or 3; ⏱8.15am-7.30pm Jun-Aug, earlier closing times rest of year) was restored by art collector Stefano Bardini (1836–1922), who purchased the land and its 17th-century villa in 1913. Beds of azaleas, peonies and wisteria bloom in April and May, irises in June. The **summer cafe** (⏱10am-6pm Apr-Sep) is a charming, albeit pricey, spot for a mid-morning coffee or tea.

❸ Picnic Provisions from ZEB

Pop into **ZEB** (www.zebgastronomia.com; Via San Miniato 2r; ⏱noon-3pm Thu & Sun-Tue, noon-3pm & 7.30-10.30pm Fri & Sat), a thoroughly modern *enoteca* (wine bar) displaying a lovely choice of traditional cold cuts at its deli-style counter, to pick up some provisions for a late-ish lunch. You'll find it in village-like San Niccolò, one of the city's most atmospheric residential pockets.

❹ Piazzale Michelangelo

Walk along Via San Miniato and up Viale Galileo Galilei to reach this vast **square** (🖥13) set atop an elevated saddle between two large public gardens, the **Giardino delle Rose** and the **Giardino dell'Iris**. The piazza offers a city panorama that is always spectacular, but is particularly dramatic at sunset.

❺ An Al Fresco Lunch

Enjoy your picnic in one of the gardens near the piazza or on the **scenic terrace** in front of the nearby Basilica di San Miniato al Monte, one of the city's oldest and most beautiful churches.

❻ Giardino Torrigiani

Backtrack to Piazza dei Pitti and make your way to this vast 19th-century **garden** (📞055 22 45 27; www.giardinotorrigiani.it; Via de' Serragli 144; 1½-hr guided tours by donation; ⏱advance reservation via email) wrapped around a 16th-century villa. Book in advance to see its rare tree species, wide English-style lawns, herb and vegetables gardens, sculpted lions and beautifully restored greenhouse. Your private tour will be conducted by the gardens' owners.

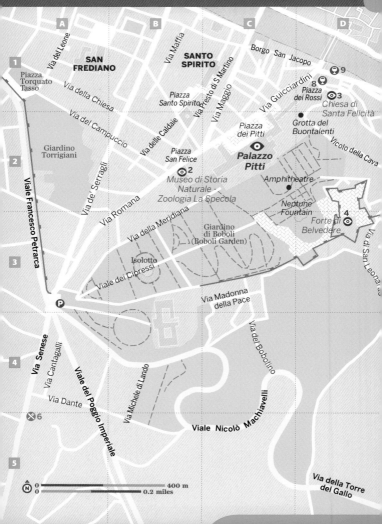

A

B

C

D

1

Via del Leone

Via Maffia

SAN FREDIANO

SANTO SPIRITO

Borgo San Jacopo

Via della Chiesa

Via Santo Spirito

Piazza Torquato Tasso

Piazza Santo Spirito

Via Presto di S. Martino

Via Guicciardini

Piazza dei Rossi

Chiesa di Santa Felicità

Via del Campuccio

Via Maggio

Via delle Caldaie

Piazza dei Pitti

Grotta del Buontalenti

2

Giardino Torrigiani

Via de' Serragli

Piazza San Felice

Museo di Storia Naturale - Zoologia La Specola

Palazzo Pitti

Amphitheatre

Vicolo della Cava

Viale Francesco Petrarca

Via Romana

Via della Meridiana

Neptune Fountain

Forte di Belvedere

3

Isolotto

Giardino di Boboli (Boboli Garden)

Viale dei Cipressi

Via Madonna della Pace

Via di San Leona

4

Via Sense

Via Cantagalli

Viale del Poggio Imperiale

Via Michele di Lando

Via del Bobolino

Via Dante

5

Viale Nicolò Machiavelli

Via della Torre del Gallo

N 0   400 m
   0   0.2 miles

E **F** **G** **H**

Via dei Molcontenti

Corso dei Tintori

Lungarno Generale Diaz

Via Tripoli

Lungarno G Pecori Giraldi

Piazza Piave

Ponte alle Grazie

Lungarno Torrigiani

Arno

Via de' Bardi

13

Piazza de' Mozzi

Piazza Nicola Demidoff

Via del Giardino Serristori

10

Via San Niccolò

Lungarno Serristori

Piazza Giuseppe Poggi

Porta San Niccolò

5

Lungarno Benvenuto Cellini

Via dei Bastioni

11

Via della Fornace

2

12

Giardino Bardini (Bardini Garden)

Piazza San Niccolò

Giardino dell'Iris

7

Viale Giuseppe Poggi

Via di Belvedere

Piazzale Michelangelo

Viale Galileo Galilei

Via di San Miniato al Monte

SAN NICCOLÒ

Via Monte alle Croci

Giardino delle Rose

3

Via dell'Erta Canina

Via della Torre del Gallo

Via delle Porte Sante

1

Basilica di San Miniato al Monte

MONTE ALLE CROCI

Viale Galileo Galilei

Via Giramonte

Viale Michelangelo

4

Via Giramontino

For reviews see	
◉ Top Sights	p100
◎ Sights	p108
✕ Eating	p109
◑ Drinking	p110
🛍 Shopping	p111

5

Sights

Basilica di San Miniato al Monte
CHURCH

1 ◉ Map p106, G4

Dedicated to St Minius, an early-Christian martyr from Florence, this Romanesque church in a spectacular location overlooking the city dates to the early 11th century, although its typically Tuscan multicoloured marble facade was tacked on a couple of centuries later. Inside, don't miss the bijou **Capella del Crocefisso**, to which Michelozzo, Agnolo Gaddi and Luca della Robbia all contributed. (www.sanminiatoalmonte.it; Via Monte alle Croce; ⊙8am-7pm May-Oct, 8am-noon & 3-6pm Nov-Apr)

Museo di Storia Naturale - Zoologia La Specola
HISTORY MUSEUM

2 ◉ Map p106, B2

One of several sections of Florence's natural history museum (established way back in 1775), La Specola showcases 5000-odd animals from its extraordinary depository of 3.5 million. The gruesome highlight – not recommended for the squeamish or young children – is the collection of wax models of bits of human anatomy in varying states of bad health. (www.msn.unifi.it; Via Romana 17; adult/reduced €6/3; ⊙9.30am-4.30pm Tue-Sun Oct-May, to 5.30pm Jun-Sep)

Chiesa di Santa Felicità
CHURCH

3 ◉ Map p106, D1

Largely a Renaissance construction, the most extraordinary feature of this church is Brunelleschi's small **Cappella Barbadori**, which is adorned by frescoes of the Annunciation by Jacopo Pontormo (1494–1557). The Corridoio Vasariano (walkway linking the Palazzo Pitti with the Uffizi) was built right across the facade so the Medicis could hear Mass like any good Christians, but without having to mix with the common folk. (www.santafelicita.it; Piazza di Santa Felicità; ⊙9.30am-noon & 3.30-5.30pm Mon-Sat)

Forte di Belvedere
FORTRESS, GALLERY

4 ◉ Map p106, D3

Designed by Bernardo Buontalenti for Grand Duke Ferdinando I at the end of the 16th century, this star-shaped fortress on one of the city's hills is only open when it hosts temporary exhibitions of contemporary art – check the website for details. Soldiers once kept watch from the massive bulwark to protect the Palazzo Pitti against foreign attack. (☎055 29 08 32; museicivicifiorentini.comune.fi.it; Via di San Leonardo 1)

Porta San Niccolò
CITY GATE

5 ◉ Map p106, G2

Built in the 1320s, the best preserved of the city's medieval gates still stands sentinel on the banks of the Arno.

Behind it, a monumental staircase designed by Giuseppe Poggi winds its way up towards Chiesa di San Miniato al Monte. (Piazza Giuseppe Poggi)

Eating

Da Ruggero
TUSCAN €€

6 Map p106, A5

A 10-minute stroll through the Boboli Garden (or along the street from Porta Romana) uncovers this trattoria, run by the gracious Corsi family since 1981 and much loved for its pure, unadulterated Florentine tradition. Cuisine is Tuscan simple and hearty – *zuppa di ortiche* (nettle soup), *spaghetti alla*

carrettiera (spaghetti in a chilli-fired tomato sauce) and of course the iconic *bistecca*. Delicious. (☑055 22 05 42; Via Senese 89r; meals €25; ☺lunch & dinner Thu-Mon, closed mid-Jul–mid-Aug)

Enoteca Fuori Porta
WINE BAR €€

7 Map p106, F2

Set just outside one of the city's medieval gates, this mellow old *enoteca* proffers up to 500 different wines, including dozens by the glass. For a light lunch or evening meal, take a seat on the pleasant terrace and order a plate or two from the limited list of pastas, salads and *crostoni* (grilled, open-faced sandwiches). (☑055 234

Chianti bottles in a Florence restaurant

24 83; www.fuoriporta.it; Via Monte alle Croci 10r; meals around €25; ☺noon-midnight daily Apr-Oct, noon-midnight Mon-Sat Jan-Mar, 7am-midnight Mon-Sat Nov-Dec; 🚍13)

and herbs), or tuck into a platter of boutique Tuscan cheeses. (www.levolpieluva. com; Piazza dei Rossi 1; crostini €6.50, cheese/meat platters €8-10; ☺11am-9pm Mon-Sat)

Drinking

Le Volpi e l'Uva   WINE BAR

8 🍷 Map p106, D1

This intimate address with marble-topped bar crowning two oak ageing wine barrels chalks up an impressive list of wines by the glass. To attain true bliss indulge in *crostoni* (€6.50) topped with honeyed speck or *lardo* (wafer-thin slices of pig fat marinated in olive oil

Open Bar   LOUNGE BAR

9 🍸 Map p106, D1

A prime location near Ponte Vecchio ensures that it's touristy, but this bar is worth a pit stop nonetheless – preferably at *aperitivo* (pre-dinner drinks accompanied by cocktail snacks) hour when chic Florentines sip cocktails, slurp oysters and enjoy the 'golden view' of the Arno swirling below their feet. (www.goldenviewopenbar.com; Via de' Bardi 58; ☺7.30am-1.30am)

LONELY PLANET/GETTY IMAGES ©

Le Volpi e l'Uva

Zoé
BAR

10 Map p106, F2

Bright, white and shiny, this savvy operation knows exactly what its hip punters want – a relaxed, faintly industrial space to hang out in all hours (well, almost). Visit for breakfast, lunch, cocktails or after-dinner party (there's often a DJ). Come springtime's warmth, the scene spills out onto a wooden decking street terrace in front. (Via dei Renai 13r; ☺8am-3am)

James Joyce
PUB

11 Map p106, H2

Neither as Irish nor as literary as the name suggests, this veteran pub with beer garden attracts a gregarious student and post-grad crowd thanks to its fabulous riverside terrace, Guinness on tap, table football and requisite U2 soundtrack. (☏055 658 08 56; Lungarno Benvenuto Cellini 1r; ☺6pm-2am Sun-Thu, 6pm-3am Fri & Sat)

Shopping

Alessandro Dari
JEWELLERY

12 Map p106, E2

Flamboyant jeweller and classical guitarist Alessandro Dari creates unique and extremely beautiful pieces in his atmospheric 15th-century workshop-showroom in San Niccolò.

Local Life
Summer Clubbing

Without a doubt the hottest and hippest place to be seen in the city on hot sultry summer nights is **Flò** (www.floifirenze.com; Piazzale Michelangelo 84; ☺7.30pm-late summer), a truly ab fab seasonal lounge bar that pops up each May or June on Piazzale Michelangelo. There are different themed lounge areas, a dance floor and a VIP area (the latter sadly restricted to the Florentine in-crowd only).

He describes his pieces as 'sculpture that you can wear' and presents them in thematic collections. (www.alessandro dari.com; Via San Niccolò 115r)

Lorenzo Villoresi
PERFUME

13 Map p106, E2

Villoresi's perfumes and potpourris meld distinctively Tuscan elements such as laurel, olive, cypress and iris with essential oils and essences from around the world. His bespoke fragrances are highly sought after. Visiting his showroom, which occupies his family's 15th-century *palazzo* (palace) is quite an experience. Drop-ins welcome but better to call in advance to arrange your visit. (☏055 234 11 87; www.lorenzovilloresi.it; Via de' Bardi 14; ☺10am-7pm Mon-Sat)

Explore

Oltrarno

Literally the 'other side of the Arno', this atmospheric neighbourhood is the traditional home of the city's artisans and its streets are studded with *botteghe* (workshops), designer boutiques and hybrid forms of both. Food is also a strength – prepared using artisanal ingredients, of course – and there's an ever-growing number of restaurants and bars to lure you across the river.

The Sights in a Day

☼ Devote your morning to exploring the area around the **Basilica di Santo Spirito** (p118), popping into the Brunelleschi-designed church and visiting local *botteghe* to watch artisans at work and to purchase hand-made items to take home as sophisticated souvenirs of your trip.

☼ For lunch, enjoy a salad or a bowl of pasta at **Tamerò** (p119) and then saunter along Via Sant'Agostino towards Piazza del Carmine to admire Masaccio's frescoes in the **Cappella Brancacci** (p118). Stop at **Gelateria Santa Trìnita** (p118) for a mid-afternoon sugar hit, and then continue up Borgo San Jacopo for some more shopping.

☾ Kick off your evening with a drink at **Il Santino** (p122), moving down a few doors to **Il Santo Bevitore** (p119) for a candlelit dinner, or heading into the residential neighbourhood of San Frediano to dine on Modern Tuscan creations at **iO Osteria Personale** (p119). Finish up enjoying live music among the bohemian crowd at **La Cité** (p123).

For a local's day in Oltrarno, see p114.

Q Local Life

City of Artisans (p114)

❤ Best of Florence

Eating
Gelateria Santa Trìnita (p118)

Il Santo Bevitore (p119)

iO Osteria Personale (p119)

Tamerò (p119)

La Casalinga (p119)

Gustapizza (p122)

Drinking
Il Santino (p122)

Volume (p115)

Vivanda (p122)

Shopping
Casini Firenze (p115)

Giulio Giannini e Figlio (p115)

Madova (p114)

Francesco da Firenze (p115)

Antico Setificio Fiorentino (p115)

Getting There

From Piazza della Stazione
Walk southeast along Via de'Panzani and Via de' Cerretani to the *duomo* (cathedral). Walk south down Via Roma, cross the Ponte Vecchio and you're in Oltrarno.

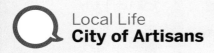

Local Life
City of Artisans

In our factory-made world, the old-fashioned *botteghe* of the Oltrarno are a particular delight. Florence's famed guilds may now be defunct, but many local artisans – welders and goldsmiths, framers and bookbinders, shoemakers and seamstresses – still hand down their craft from generation to generation on this side of the Arno.

❶ A Pair of Gloves from Madova
The Donnini family has been producing leather gloves since 1919 and selling them from this **shop** (www.madova. com; Via Guicciardini 1r; ⊙10am-7pm Mon-Sat) since 1954. The gloves can come in every colour and type of leather you desire, lined with cashmere, silk or lambs wool.

2 Giulio Giannini e Figlio –
Bookbinding Legends

One of Florence's oldest artisan families, the Gianninis have made and sold marbled paper, beautifully bound books and stationery from this **shop** (www.giuliogiannini.it; Piazza Pitti 37r; ⏰10am-7pm Mon-Sat, 11am-6.30pm Sun) since 1856. Don't miss the upstairs workshop.

3 Leather Fashion

The Tattanelli family business started in 1945 with quality leather bags, wallets and attache cases, but branched out into leather clothing in 1971 when this boutique, **Casini Firenze** (www.casinifirenze.it; Piazza Pitti 30-31r; ⏰10am-7pm Mon-Sat, 11am-6pm Sun), first opened. It's a great place to source men's and women's bags, shoes, belts and ready-to-wear clothing.

4 A Modern Design Atelier

The creation of Simafra Prosperi, a young Florentine painter, decorator and art restorer, **La Bottega Moderna** (www.labottegamoderna.com; Via Romana 118r; ⏰10am-1pm & 3.30-7.30pm Wed-Sat) is a modern take on a traditional artist's workshop. It stocks a mix of design objects, art works and decorative pieces for the home, many made from recycled or upcycled objects.

5 Artisanal Ingredients

Backtrack into the heart of Santo Spirito to investigate the hand-cured meats, conserved truffles, artisanal cheese, wood-fired bread and other delicatessen products sold at **Olio & Convivium** (☎055 265 81 98; www.conviviumfirenze.it; Via di Santo Spirito 4; meals €35; ⏰lunch & dinner Tue-Sat, lunch Mon). Stock up on supplies at the front counter, or dine out back.

6 Shoes from Francesco da Firenze

Hand-stitched leather is the cornerstone of this tiny family **business** (www.francescodafirenze.it; Via di Santo Spirito 62r; ⏰10am-7pm Mon-Sat, closed 2 weeks Aug) specialising in gorgeous ready-to-wear and made-to-measure men's and women's shoes; some models on offer are *pezzi unici* (unique pieces).

7 Traditional Florentine Fabrics

The master weavers of **Antico Setificio Fiorentino** (Via Bartolini 4; ⏰9am-1pm & 2-5pm Mon-Fri) produce traditional Florentine fabrics, brocades and damasks on 12 looms: six handlooms from the 18th century and six semi-mechanical looms from the 19th century. Head here to buy fabric or to browse accessories made from hand-woven silk.

8 An Artisan's Watering Hole

Celebrate a successful day's shopping at **Volume** (www.volumefirenze.com; Piazza Santo Spirito 3r; ⏰9am-1.30am), a hybrid cafe-bar-gallery in an old hat-making *bottega* (workshop) on Piazza Santo Spirito. This area is where many of the local artisans come to enjoy a drink at the end of the day, so you're sure to be alongside some of them.

Piazza di Verzaia

Sabatino (50m)

6 ✕ A 1

Via San Giovanni

Piazza dei Nerli

Piazza di Cestello C

Lungarno Guicciardini D

SAN FREDIANO

Via del Drago d'Oro

Via del Leone

Borgo San Frediano

19 ☆

13 ✕

Piazza N Sauro

14 ✕

✕ 11 Via dell'Orto

Piazza del Carmine

17 🚇

Borgo della Stella

18 🚇

Piazza Piattellina

1 ◉ Cappella Brancacci

Via Santa Monaca

16 🚇

Via di Camaldoli

Via del Leone

Piazza Torquato Tasso

Via dell'Ardiglione

Via de' Serragli

Via Sant'Agostino

Via Maffia

Viale Francesco Petrarca

Via della Chiesa

Giardino Torrigiani

Via del Campuccio

Via delle Caldaie

Via Santa Maria

Giardino Torrigiani

3 ◉

To Piazzale Porta Romana (300m)

For reviews see

◉	Sights	p118
✕	Eating	p119
🚇	Drinking	p122
☆	Entertainment	p123
🔒	Shopping	p123

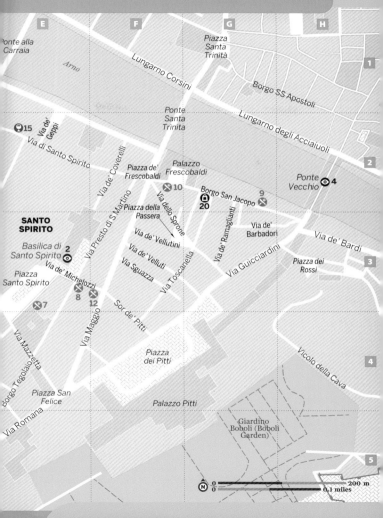

E

F

G

H

1

Ponte alla Carraia

Arno

Lungarno Corsini

Piazza Santa Trinità

Borgo SS Apostoli

Ponte Santa Trinità

Lungarno degli Acciaiuoli

2

15

Via de' Geppi

Via di Santo Spirito

Via di Coverelli

Piazza de' Frescobaldi

Palazzo Frescobaldi

Ponte Vecchio

4

10

Borgo San Jacopo

9

20

SANTO SPIRITO

Via Presto di S. Martino

Piazza della Passera

Via dello Sprone

Via de' Vellutini

Via de' Ramaglianti

Via de' Barbadori

Via de' Bardi

Basilica di Santo Spirito

2

Via de' Velluti

Via Sguazza

Via Toscanella

Via Guicciardini

Piazza dei Rossi

3

Piazza Santo Spirito

Via de' Michelozzi

8

12

7

Via Maggio

Sor de' Pitti

Piazza dei Pitti

Vicolo della Cava

4

Via Mazzetta

Borgo Tegolaio

Piazza San Felice

Via Romana

Palazzo Pitti

Giardino Boboli (Boboli Garden)

5

N

0   200 m
0   0.1 miles

Sights

Cappella Brancacci CHAPEL

1 ◎ Map p116, C2

Part of **Basilica di Santa Maria del Carmine** (enter through the door to the right), this chapel is home to Masaccio's famous fresco cycle illustrating the life of St Peter. Highlights are *The Expulsion of Adam and Eve from Paradise* and *The Tribute Money* panels. Visits are by guided tour (20 minutes, every 20 minutes); numbers are restricted and reservations recommended. (☑055 276 82 24; www.musefirenze.it; Piazza del Carmine 14; adult/reduced €6/4.50; ☺10am-4.30pm Wed-Sat & Mon, 1-4.30pm Sun)

Basilica di Santo Spirito CHURCH

2 ◎ Map p116, E3

The facade of this Brunelleschi-designed basilica presides over Florence's most shabby-chic piazza. Inside, 38 semicircular chapels and a colonnade of grey *pietra forte* (ochre-coloured sandstone) Corinthian columns inject monumental grandeur. Don't miss the **sacristy** and its poignant wooden crucifix attributed by some experts to Michelangelo; access is through the door next to the Cappella Segni in the left aisle. (Piazza Santo Spirito; ☺8.30am-12.30pm & 4-5.30pm Thu-Tue)

Giardino Torrigiani GARDEN

3 ◎ Map p116, C5

Behind the unassuming facades of Via de' Serragli lies this vast 19th-century garden, a privately owned oasis featuring rare tree species, wide English-style lawns, herb and vegetables gardens, sculpted lions and a beautifully restored greenhouse. Guided tours (in English or Italian) are intimate and proffer a rare glimpse into a very different and privileged Florentine world. (☑055 22 45 27; www.giardinotorrigiani.it; Via de' Serragli 144; 1½-hr guided tours by donation; ☺advance reservation via email)

Ponte Vecchio BRIDGE

4 ◎ Map p116, H2

Florence's iconic bridge dates from 1345 and has twinkled with the glittering wares of jewellers ever since the 16th century, when Ferdinando I de'Medici ordered them here to replace the often malodorous presence of Florence's butchers. Above the shops on the eastern side is the infamous **Corridoio Vasariano**,

---

Local Life
Gelateria Santa Trinita

A prominent location just off the Ponte Santa Trinita is but one of the reasons for the huge popularity of this **gelateria** (Map p116, F2; www.gelateriasantatrinita.it; Piazza Frescobaldi 11-12r; ☺11.30am-11pm) – its ultracreamy gelato and flavourful sorbet are others (opt for the Bronte pistachio or any of the fresh-fruit flavours). Join the locals in enjoying your cone or cup by the side of the Arno.

built around – rather than straight through – a medieval tower at the bridge's southern end.

Eating

Il Santo Bevitore

MODERN TUSCAN €€

5 🍴 Map p116, D2

Reserve or arrive dot-on 7.30pm to snag the last dinner table at this raved-about address, an ode to style where gastronomes dine in a vaulted, whitewashed, bottle-lined interior. The menu is a creative reinvention of seasonal classics, different for lunch and dinner. (☑055 21 12 64; www.ilsantobevitore.com; Via di Santo Spirito 64-66r; meals €35; ☺lunch & dinner Sep-Jul)

iO Osteria Personale

MODERN TUSCAN €€€

6 🍴 Map p116, A1

Persuade everyone at your table to order the tasting menu to avoid the torture of picking just one dish – everything at this creative place is to die for. Chef Nicolò Baretti uses only seasonal products, natural ingredients and traditional flavours – to sensational effect. (☑055 933 13 41; www.io-osteriapersonale.it; Borgo San Frediano 167r; meals €45; ☺dinner from 8pm Mon-Sat)

Tamerò

PASTA BAR €

7 🍴 Map p116, E3

A happening address on Florence's hippest square: admire pasta cooks at work in the open kitchen while you

wait for a table – you'll probably have to. A party-loving crowd flocks here for imaginative, fresh pasta dishes (€7.50 to €10), giant salads (€7.50) and copious cheese/salami platters (€9). Weekend DJs spin sets from 10pm. (☑055 28 25 96; www.tamero.it; Piazza Santa Spirito 11r; meals €20; ☺lunch & dinner Tue-Sun)

La Casalinga

TRATTORIA €

8 🍴 Map p116, E3

Locally loved, this busy, unpretentious place is one of Florence's cheapest trattorias. Don't be surprised if Paolo, the patriarch figure who conducts the show from behind the bar, relegates you behind locals in the queue: it's a fact of life. Eventually, you'll be rewarded with hearty Tuscan dishes cooked to exacting perfection. (☑055 21 86 24; www.trattorialacasalinga.it; Via de' Michelozzi 9r; meals €25; ☺lunch & dinner Mon-Sat)

Il Ristoro

TUSCAN €

9 Map p116, G2

This two-room restaurant with deli counter is a great budget choice – its two-course €15 lunch deal is a steal. Pick from classics like *pappa al pomodoro* (thick bread and tomato soup) or a plate of cold cuts, and swoon at views of the Arno swirling beneath your feet. (☎055 264 55 69; ilristorodeiper ditempo.it; Borgo San Jacopo 48r; meals €20; ☺noon-4pm Mon, to 10pm Tue-Sun)

Trattoria Camillo

TRATTORIA €€€

10 Map p116, F2

Crostini (toasts with various toppings) topped with aphrodisiacal white-truffle shavings, deep-fried battered green tomatoes or zucchini (courgette) flowers and homemade walnut liqueur are a few of the seasonal highlights served beneath a centuries-old red-brick vaulted ceiling at this much-loved trattoria. Exceptional quality and endearingly old-fashioned service. (☎055 21 24 27; Borgo San Jacopo 57r; meals €50; ☺lunch & dinner Thu-Mon)

Il Guscio

TUSCAN €€€

11 Map p116, A2

Exceptional dishes come out of the kitchen of this family-run gem in San Frediano, which is greatly loved by locals. Meat and fish are given joint billing on the menu; the offerings are

Typical Florentine trattoria

ATLANTIDE PHOTOTRAVEL/CORBIS ©

Understand

Gourmet Florence

Be it by sinking your teeth into a flavoursome *bistecca alla fiorentina* (T-bone steak), savouring the taste and aroma of freshly shaved white truffles or sampling rustic specialities such as *trippa alla fiorentina* (tripe slow cooked with onion, carrot, celery and tomatoes), you're sure to discover plenty of taste sensations when eating in Florence.

The cuisine here has stayed faithful to its humble regional roots, relying on fresh local produce and eschewing fussy execution. That's not to say that it lacks refinement – Florence is home to many highly skilled and internationally lauded chefs – but it's true to say that the hallmark of the local cuisine is its simplicity.

When here, be sure to try a *bistecca alla fiorentina,* but be prepared for it to come to the table *al sangue* (bloody). Accompanied by slow-cooked white beans, or sometimes roast potatoes, this signature dish relies on the quality of its Chianina beef (from the Val di Chiana south of Florence) and the skill with which it has been butchered and grilled. Wash it down with a Tuscan red wine – a Chianti Classico, Brunello di Montepulciano or perhaps even a Vino Nobile di Montepulciano.

Other local specialities include *cinghiale* (wild boar), best savoured in autumnal stews; antipasti plates featuring fresh pecorino cheese made from sheep's milk, locally cured meats and *crostini* (lightly toasted pieces of bread topped with liver pate); and *minestre* (soups) including *zuppa di fagioli* (bean soup), *ribollita* (a 'reboiled' bean, vegetable and bread soup with black cabbage) and *pappa al pomodoro* (a thick bread and tomato soup).

Adventurous eaters need go no further than the city's *trippai* (tripe carts), where tripe *panini* (sandwiches) are doused in *salsa verde* (a tasty pea-green sauce of smashed parsley, garlic, capers and anchovies). Such rustic, powerfully flavoured treats stand in stark contrast to the refined joy of white truffles from San Miniato near Pisa – best shaved over a bowl of pasta or risotto – and porcini mushrooms gathered in local forests and tossed through *taglierini* (thin ribbon pasta). Both of these indulgences are surprisingly affordable and utterly delectable.

always tasty and often inspired. (☎055 22 44 21; www.il-guscio.it; Via dell'Orto 49; meals €40; ☺lunch & dinner Mon-Sat)

Gustapizza   PIZZERIA €

12 ✕ Map p116, F3

Order your pizza at the counter and then take a seat at one of the glass-topped wine casks that serve as tables at this newish spot a block off Piazza Santo Spirito. Service is brusque but the pizza, with its medium-to-thick crust baked in a traditional wood oven, is unimpeachably good. (Via Maggio 46r; pizza €4.50-8; ☺11.30am-3pm & 7-11pm Tue-Sun)

Momoyama   JAPANESE €€€

13 ✕ Map p116, D1

When the urge for a pasta-free evening kicks in, head here. This thoroughly contemporary designer

---

Local Life
Piazza del Passera

This bijou square (Map p116, F2) with no passing traffic is a gourmet gem. Pick from cheap wholesome tripe in various guises at **Il Magazzino** (☎055 21 59 69; www.trippe riailmagazzino.com; Piazza della Passera 2/3; meals €30; ☺lunch & dinner), or pricier Tuscan classics at **Trattoria 4 Leoni** (☎055 21 85 62; www.4leoni. com; Piazza della Passera 2/3; meals €40; ☺lunch & dinner) known for its *bistecca alla fiorentina* (chargrilled T-bone steak) that it has cooked up since 1550; reservations essential.

---

noodle bar cooks up beautifully sculpted platters of sushi, sashami, carpaccio, rolls and a creative selection of noodle bowls. Late opening hours cater to the chic party set. (☎055 29 18 40; www.ristorantemomoyama. it; Borgo San Frediano 10r; meals €40; ☺12.30-2.30pm & 7.30pm-2am)

La Carraia   GELATO €

14 ✕ Map p116, D1

Take one look at the constant queue out the door of this bright green-and-citrus shop with its exciting flavours and you'll know you're at a real Florentine favourite. Ricotta and pear, anyone? (Piazza Nazario Sauro 25r; ☺9am-11pm summer, to 10pm winter)

Drinking

Il Santino   WINE BAR

15 🍷 Map p116, E2

Run by the gastronomic young guns from Il Santo Bevitore, this pocket-sized wine bar is packed out every evening. Inside, squat modern stools contrast with old brick walls but from 9pm the action spills onto the street. (Via Santo Spirito 34; glass of wine & crostini €6.50-8; ☺10am-10pm)

Vivanda   WINE BAR

16 🍷 Map p116, D3

A first for gourmet Florence, the focus of this bright modern *enoteca* (wine bar) – its small interior packed cheek by jowl with tables – is organic wine. Locally sourced products ensure a delightful lunch, or reserve in advance for an early-evening tasting (€25) – four different organic wines perfectly paired with ash-aged *pecorino* (sheep's milk cheese), *ricotta di bufala* and Cinta Senese (Tuscan pig) salami. (www.vivandafirenze.it; Via Santa Monaca 7r; meals €25; ☺lunch & dinner)

Dolce Vita
BAR

17 🚇 Map p116, C2

This '80s favourite hosts live bands and small photography/art exhibitions in its small, design-driven interior. The action spills onto a decking terrace in summer. (www.dolcevitaflorence.com; Piazza del Carmine 6r; ☺5pm-2am Tue-Sun, closed 2 weeks Aug)

Cuculia
CAFE

18 🍽 Map p116, D2

This hybrid bookshop-cafe is a serene spot to while away a few hours in the company of classical music and shelves loaded with books. The vibe is old-world refinement and the tiny candlelit nook out back is perfect for a romantic moment over a cocktail. Food too. (www.cuculia.it; Via dei Serragli 11; ☺10am-midnight Tue-Fri, 10am-1am Sat)

Entertainment

La Cité
LIVE MUSIC

19 ⭐ Map p116, D1

By day this cafe-bookshop is a hip cappuccino stop with vintage seating to flop down on and surf. By night

Basilica di Santo Spirito (p118)

(from 10pm) the intimate bookshelf-lined space morphs into a vibrant live music spot: think swing, fusion and jam-session jazz. (www.lacitelibreria.info; Borgo San Frediano 20r; ☺3pm-1am Mon-Thu, 5pm-2am Fri & Sat; 🛜)

Shopping

Obsequium
WINE

20 🔒 Map p116, G2

Occupying the ground floor of one of the city's best-preserved medieval towers, this shop offers a wide range of fine Tuscan wines, wine accessories and gourmet foods, including truffles. (www.obsequium.it; Borgo San Jacopo 17-39r; ☺11am-7.30pm)

Explore

Pisa

Once a maritime power to rival Genoa and Venice, Pisa now draws its fame from an architectural project gone terribly wrong. But the world-famous Leaning Tower is just one of many noteworthy sights in this compact and compelling city. Romanesque buildings, Gothic churches and Renaissance piazzas abound, and there's also a vibrant and affordable cafe and bar scene.

The Sights in a Day

☀ Kick-start your Pisan peregrination in Borgo Stretto, the city's medieval heart, with a coffee and sweet treat at the bar of historic **Salza** (p133). Then wander alongside the Arno to visit the **Museo Nazionale di San Matteo** (p131) with its rich collection of painting and sculpture from the Tuscan school.

☀ For lunch, make your choice from the small but delectable menu at **Osteria Bernardo** (p132) and then head to the city's major attraction, **Piazza dei Miracoli** (p126). Organise your ticket to the Leaning Tower, then start your three-hour exploration of it, the *duomo* (cathedral) *battistero* (baptistry), Camposanto and museums – make sure you see them all!

☾ Head back towards the train station via handsome Piazza dei Cavalieri with its magnificent *palazzi* (palaces) and bustling bar scene. Stop here to enjoy an *aperitivo* (pre-dinner drinks accompanied by cocktail snacks), or continue to one of the bars in **Piazza delle Vettovaglie** (p132) or to hipster favourite, **Keith** (p133), overlooking the Haring mural. End your visit by watching the sun set over the Arno.

👁 **Top Sights**

Piazza dei Miracoli (p126)

❤ **Best of Florence**

Art
Museo Nazionale di San Matteo (p131)

Museo dell'Opera del Duomo (p128)

Battistero (p127)

Eating
Osteria Bernardo (p132)

Il Montino (p132)

Il Crudo (p132)

Drinking
Keith (p133)

Sottobosco (p133)

Salza (p133)

Getting There

🚆 **Train** Regular services leave Florence (€7, 1¼ hours) for the conveniently located Pisa Centrale station.

🚗 **Car** Take the toll-free SCG FI-PI-LI (SS67) from Florence. Street parking costs €2 per hour, but you must be careful to stay outside the city's Limited Traffic Zone (ZTL). There's a free car park outside the zone on Lungarno Guadalongo.

Top Sights
Piazza dei Miracoli

No Tuscan sight is more immortalised in kitsch souvenirs than the iconic tower teetering on the edge of this famous piazza, also known as Piazza del Duomo (Cathedral Sq). Its expansive green lawns provide an urban carpet on which Europe's most extraordinary concentration of Romanesque buildings – in the form of *duomo* (cathedral), *battistero* (baptistry) and *campanile* (bell tower) – are arranged. Despite all the tourist hype, it truly does live up to its commonly used name, the *Campo dei Miracoli* (Field of Miracles).

Campo dei Miracoli

◉ Map p130, B1

www.opapisa.it

Leaning Tower of Pisa

Don't Miss

Leaning Tower

Yes, it's true: Pisa's famous **tower** (Torre Pendente; Map p130; incl admission to cathedral €18; ☺10am-4.30pm Dec & Jan, 9.40am-4.30pm Nov & Feb, 9am-5.30pm Mar, 8.30am-8pm Apr-Sep, 9am-6.30pm Oct) really does lean. The steep climb up its 300-odd steps is strenuous and can be tricky (children under eight are not admitted; those aged eight to 12 years must hold an adult's hand), but the views from the top make it well worthwhile.

Duomo

Pisa's huge 11th-century **cathedral** (Map p130; admission free with ticket for one of the other Piazza dei Miracoli sights or with coupon from ticket office; ☺10am-12.45pm & 2-4.30pm Jan-Feb & Nov-Dec, to 5.30pm Mar, to 7.30pm Apr-Sep, to 6.30pm Oct) with its striking cladding of green and cream marble (a 13th-century addition) was the blueprint for Romanesque churches throughout Tuscany. The elliptical dome, the first of its kind in Europe at the time, dates from 1380 and the wooden ceiling decorated with 24-carat gold is a legacy of Medici rule.

Giovanni Pisano's Pulpit

The extraordinary octagonal pulpit in the north aisle was sculpted from Carrara marble by Pisano between 1302 and 1310; it was inspired by his father's pulpit in the *battistero* and also features nude and heroic figures. With it, Pisano brought a new pictorial expressionism and life to Gothic sculpture.

Battistero

Construction of the cupcake-style **baptistry** (Map p130; Piazza dei Miracoli; combination ticket Battistero, Camposanto, Museo dell'Opera del Duomo & Museo delle Sinópie 1/2/3/4 sights €5/7/8/9, reduced €3/4/5/6;

☑ Top Tips

► There are limited admissions to the Leaning Tower: book the first available slot as soon as you arrive; ticket desks are behind the tower and in the Museo delle Sinópie. Or book in advance online (but note tickets can only be bought 12 to 20 days before visiting).

► Admission to the *duomo* is free, but you need to show a ticket – either for one of the other sights or a *duomo* coupon distributed at ticket offices.

► From 16 June until the last Sunday in August or first in September, the Leaning Tower and Camposanta open until 9.30pm.

✗ Take a Break

► Pick up a *cecina* (chickpea pizza) or a *focaccine* (small flat roll) from Il Montino (p132).

► For a sightseeing coffee break, it's worth making the short trek to Salza (p133).

🕙10am-4.30pm Jan-Feb & Nov-Dec, 9am-5.30pm Mar, 8am-7.30pm Apr-Sep, 9am-6.30pm Oct) began in 1152, but the building was remodelled and continued by Nicola and Giovanni Pisano more than a century later and finally completed in the 14th century. Don't leave without climbing to the Upper Gallery to listen to the custodian demonstrate the double dome's remarkable acoustics and echo effects.

Nicola Pisano's Pulpit

Inside the *battistero*, a hexagonal marble pulpit (1260) by Nicola Pisano is the undoubted highlight. Inspired by the Roman sarcophagi in the Camposanto, Pisano used powerful classical models to enact scenes from biblical legend. His figure of Daniel, who supports one of the corners of the pulpit on his shoulders, is particularly extraordinary.

Museo dell'Opera del Duomo

This **museum** (Map p130; Piazza dei Miracoli; combination ticket Battistero, Camposanto, Museo dell'Opera del Duomo & Museo delle Sinópie 1/2/3/4 sights €5/7/8/9, reduced €3/4/5/6; 🕙10am-4.30pm Jan-Feb & Nov-Dec, 9am-5.30pm Mar, 8am-7.30pm Apr-Sep, 9am-6.30pm Oct) is a repository for works of art once displayed in the *duomo* and *battistero*, including Giovanni Pisano's ivory carving of the Madonna and Child (1299), made for the *duomo*'s high altar, and a carved griffin that once crowned its dome. Don't miss the tranquil cloister garden

with its great views of the Leaning Tower.

Camposanto

Soil shipped from Calvary during the Crusades is said to lie within the white walls of this hauntingly beautiful cloistered **quadrangle** (Map p130; Piazza dei Miracoli; combination ticket Battistero, Camposanto, Museo dell'Opera del Duomo & Museo delle Sinópie 1/2/3/4 sights €5/7/8/9, reduced €3/4/5/6; 🕙10am-4.30pm Jan-Feb & Nov-Dec, 9am-5.30pm Mar, 8am-7.30pm Apr-Sep, 9am-6.30pm Oct) where prominent Pisans were once buried. Some of the sarcophagi here are of Graeco-Roman origin, recycled during the Middle Ages. During WW2, Allied artillery unfortunately destroyed many of the 14th- and 15th-century frescoes that once covered the cloister walls.

The Triumph of Death

Among the few of the Camposanto's frescoes to survive was this remarkable illustration of Hell (1333–41) attributed to Buonamico Buffalmacco. Fortunately, the mirrors once stuck next to the graphic images of the damned being roasted alive on spits have been removed – originally, viewers would have seen their own faces in the horrific scene.

Museo delle Sinópie

This **museum** (Map p130; Piazza dei Miracoli; combination ticket Battistero, Camposanto, Museo dell'Opera del Duomo &

Camposanto, Piazza dei Miracoli

Museo delle Sinópie 1/2/3/4 sights €5/7/8/9, reduced €3/4/5/6; ⊙10am-4.30pm Jan-Feb & Nov-Dec, 9am-5.30pm Mar, 8am-7.30pm Apr-Sep, 9am-6.30pm Oct) safeguards several *sinópie* (preliminary sketches) drawn by artists in red-earth pigment on the walls of the Camposanto in the 14th and 15th centuries before frescoes were painted over them. It offers a compelling study in fresco painting technique, with short films and scale models filling in the gaps.

Camposanto

Battistero Duomo Leaning
Tower

Via Contessa Matilde

Strada Statale

To A11; A1
FI-PI-
Lucca (25k

**Piazza dei
Miracoli** ◉

Museo
dell'Opera
del Duomo

Via Cardinale Maffi

Via San Zeno

*Museo delle
Sinópie*

Piazza
Arcivescovado

Via
Capponi

Piazza
P Santa Caterina

Via Buonarroti

Via Roma

Via Don G Boschi

Via Santa Maria

Via della Faggiola

Piazza Martiri
della Libertà

Via Carducci

Via Salvi

Piazza
Cavallotti

Via
Corsica

Piazza dei
Cavalieri

Via Oberdan

Via Santa Cecilia

Via Fucini

Via San Lorenzo

Via Volta

Orto
Botanico

Via Santa Maria

Via Paoli

Piazza San
Omobono

9

Via San Francesco

Via Sant'Andrea

Via de Simone

For reviews see
◉ Top Sights   p126
◉ Sights   p131
✗ Eating   p132
🅟 Drinking   p133

Piazza
Dante
Alighieri

Via San Frediano

6 ✗

12

Borgo Stretto

10 ✗

Via Cavour

5

Piazza
San Paolo
all'Orto

Via Palestro

8

Lungarno Pacinotti

Arno

11

Piazza delle
Vettovaglie

✗

Via delle
Calafati

Via San Martino

Via Sant'Andrea

Piazza
Garibaldi

7

Ponte di
Mezzo

Piazza
Cairoli

Via delle
Belle Torri

Piazza
Mazzini Muse
Nazionale
San Matte

Ponte
Solferino

Lungarno Gambacorti

Palazzo
Blu

Lungarno Mediceo

Piazza San
Matteo in
Soarta

Chiesa di Santa
Maria della Spina

3

Lungarno Simonelli

Ponta del
Fortezz

Lungarno Sonnino

Viale Crispi

Via Sant'Antonio

Via Mazzini

Corso Italia

Via San Martino

Lungarno Galilei

Piazza San
Martino

Filbonacci

Via Niosi

Via Manzoni

Piazza
M D'Azeglio

Via del Carmine

Via Pascoli

Via Ceci

Via Nino Bixio

Piazza
Sant'Antonio

Via
Mazzini

4

Domus
Mazziniana

◉

Via
Zandonai

Piazza
Vittorio
Emanuele II

Viale Croce

Piazza
Guerrazzi

Lungarno Guadalonga

Via Cesare Battisti

🅟

Ⓝ 0   200 m
   0   0.1 miles

Piazza della
Stazione

Stazione Pisa
Centrale

To Pisa
International
Airport (2.4km)

Chiesa di Santa Maria della Spina

Sights

Museo Nazionale di San Matteo

ART GALLERY

1 ⊙ Map p130, D3

This inspiring repository of medieval masterpieces sits in a 13th-century Benedictine convent. The collection of paintings from the Tuscan school (c 12th to 14th centuries) is notable, with works by Lippo Memmi, Taddeo Gaddi, Gentile da Fabriano and Ghirlandaio. Don't miss Masaccio's *St Paul,* Fra Angelico's *Madonna of Humility* and Simone Martini's *Polyptych of Saint Catherine.* (Piazza San Matteo in Soarta; adult/reduced €2.50; ⊘8.30am-7pm Tue-Sat, to 1.30pm Sun)

Chiesa di Santa Maria della Spina

CHURCH

2 ⊙ Map p130, B3

A fine example of Pisan-Gothic style, this now-decommissioned church, built in 1230, was originally called Santa Maria di Pontenovo. In 1333 it acquired a reliquary of a *spina* (thorn) from Christ's crown and was renamed as a result. Its ornately spired exterior is encrusted with tabernacles and statues. At the time of research the interior was closed to the public. (Lungarno Gambacorti)

Palazzo Blu ART GALLERY

3 💿 Map p130, C3

This magnificently restored, 14th-century building has a striking dusty-blue facade. Inside, its over-the-top 19th-century interior houses the Foundation CariPisa's art collection – predominantly Pisan works from the 14th to the 20th centuries – as well as temporary exhibitions. (www.palazzoblu.it; Lungarno Gambacorti 9; admission free; ⏱10am-7pm Tue-Fri, to 8pm Sat & Sun)

Domus Mazziniana MUSEUM

4 💿 Map p130, B4

With a beautiful, renovated facade, Palazzo Nathan-Rosselli, the Pisan *domus* (large house) where Italian revolutionary and champion of Italian unification Giuseppe Mazzini died in 1872, holds artifacts that document Mazzinian and democratic ideology during the Risorgimento (reunification period). (www.domusmazziniana.it; Via Mazzini 71; admission free; ⏱9am-12.30pm Mon-Fri)

Q Local Life
Piazza delle Vettovaglie

This atmospheric **piazza** (Map p130, C3) hosts a bustling fresh-produce market during the day, but is even busier at night, when patrons (including many of the city's elite universities) spill out of its many bars, cafes and restaurants to party under the 15th-century porticoes.

Eating

Osteria Bernardo MODERN TUSCAN €€

5 🍴 Map p130, D3

This small *osteria* (tavern) well away from the madding Leaning Tower crowd is the perfect fusion of easy dining and gourmet excellence. Its menu is small – just four or five dishes to choose from for each course – and the cuisine is creative. (☎050 57 52 16; www.osteriabernardo.it; Piazza San Paolo all'Orto 1; meals €30; ⏱lunch & dinner Tue-Sun)

Il Montino PIZZERIA €

6 🍴 Map p130, C3

At this down-to-earth and much-loved pizzeria, take away or grab a table (order at the bar) to enjoy house specialities such as *cecina* and *spuma* (sweet, nonalcoholic drink). Or go for a *focaccine* (small flat roll) filled with salami, pancetta or *porchetta* (suckling pig). Look for the blue neon 'Pizzeria' sign. (Vicolo del Monte 1; pizzas €3-6.50; ⏱10.30am-3pm & 5-10pm Mon-Sat)

Il Crudo SANDWICHES €

7 🍴 Map p130, C3

Choose a well-filled *panino* (sandwich) to munch on the move or enjoy one alfresco with a glass of wine at this pocket-sized *panineria* (sandwich shop) and *vineria* (wine bar) strung with ham legs. Find it by the river on one of Pisa's prettiest squares. (www.ilcrudopisa.it; Piazza Cairoli 7; panini €4.50-6;

🕐11am-3.30pm & 5pm-1am Mon-Thu, to 2am Fri, to 2am Sat, to 1am Sun)

Osteria del Porton Rosso

OSTERIA €€

8 🍴 Map p130, C3

Don't be put off by the dank alley; inside it's all style, charm and excellent regional cuisine. Pisan specialities such as fresh ravioli with salted cod and chickpeas happily coexist with Tuscan classics such as grilled fillet steak. The €10 lunchtime deal offers unbeatable value. (🕿050 58 05 66; www.portonrosso.com; Vicolo del Porton Rosso 11; meals €25; 🕐lunch & dinner Mon-Sat)

biOsteria 050

ORGANIC €€

9 🍴 Map p130, D2

Everything that Zero Cinquanta (050) cooks up is strictly seasonal, local and organic. All products are sourced from farms within a 50km radius of Pisa. A simple but satisfying menu, with ample choice for vegetarians and coeliacs too. The daily lunch specials are particularly good value. (🕿050 54 31 06; Via San Francesco 36; meals €20-30; 🕐lunch Mon-Sun, dinner Tue-Sun; 🎋)

Drinking

Sottobosco

CAFE

10 🍺 Map p130, C3

A bohemian cafe with a few books for sale and vintage-themed decor. A laid-back choice for a coffee, light lunch or drink. At dusk, jazz bands play or DJs

🔵 Local Life
Art Play

American pop artist Keith Haring painted *Tuttomondo* (1989) on a convent facade in Pisa months before his untimely death in 1990. Hip cafe–art shop **Keith** (Map p130, B4; www.keithcafe.com; Via Zandonai 4; 🕐7am-11pm; 📶) sits opposite; sip a cocktail on the terrace and ponder Haring's 30 signature prancing, dancing men. Free wi-fi, art exhibitions, knitting evenings, puzzle nights, superb coffee and one of the funkiest outdoor spaces in town ensure this place buzzes.

spin tunes. (www.sottoboscocafe.it; Piazza San Paolo all'Orto; 🕐10am-midnight Tue-Fri, noon-1am Sat, 7pm-midnight Sun)

Bazeel

BAR

11 🍺 Map p130, C3

Generous *aperitivo* spread, live music or DJs, and a great little terrace out front. Check its Twitter feed for what's on. (www.bazeel.it; Lungarno Pacinotti 1; 🕐5pm-2am)

Salza

CAFE

12 🍺 Map p130, C3

This old-fashioned cake shop has been tempting Pisans since 1898. An equally good spot for a cocktail – anytime. Prop at the bar or at tables in the arcade. (Borgo Stretto 44; 🕐8am-8.30pm summer, shorter hr Tue-Sun winter)

Top Sights
Lucca

Getting There

🚃 Regional services from Florence (€7, 1¼ to 1¾ hours, hourly). From the train station, follow the path across the moat.

🚗 A11 from Florence. Park at Parcheggio Carducci, just outside Porta Sant'Anna.

Hidden behind imposing Renaissance walls, the pedestrianised cobbled streets, handsome piazzas and shady promenades of Lucca's *centro storico* (historic centre) make it is easy to explore on foot. The city is proud possessor of a stunning group of Romanesque churches – look for the Cattedrale di San Martino, the Chiesa di San Michele in Foro, the Chiesa di San Paolino, the Basilica di San Frediano and the Chiesa e Battistero dei SS Giovanni e Reparata.

Views over Lucca

Don't Miss

City Wall

Lucca's monumental *mura* (wall; 12m high, 4km long) was built around the old city in the 16th and 17th centuries and remains in almost perfect condition. Its ramparts are crowned with a tree-lined footpath that is a favourite Lucchesi location for a *passeggiata* (evening stroll), bike ride or picnic. **Biciclette Poli** and **Cicli Bizzarri** on Piazza Santa Maria hire bikes (per day €15; 9am to 7pm summer) as does the tourist office in Piazzale Verdi.

Cattedrale di San Martino

This predominantly Romanesque **cathedral** (Piazza San Martino; ☉ 7am-6pm summer, to 5pm winter; sacristy 9.30am-4.45pm Mon-Fri, 9.30am-6.45pm Sat, 11.30am-5pm Sun; sacristy adult/reduced €3/2, with cathedral museum & Chiesa dei SS Giovanni e Reparata €7/5) dates to the start of the 11th century. Inside, the **Volto Santo** is a simply fashioned Christ on a wooden crucifix that dates from the 13th century.

Memorial to Ilaria del Carretto

Enter the cathedral's **sacristy** to admire this gleaming marble memorial, carved by Jacopo della Quercia in 1407. The young second wife of a 15th-century lord of Lucca, Ilaria died in childbirth aged 24. At her feet lies her faithful dog.

Palazzo Pfanner

Take a stroll around this beautiful, 17th-century **palace** (www.palazzopfanner.it; Via degli Asili 33; palace or garden adult/reduced €4.50/4, both €6/5; ☉10am-6pm summer) where parts of Jane Campion's *The Portrait of a Lady* (1996) were shot. Highlights include the frescoed and furnished *piano nobile* (main reception room) and the gorgeous, baroque-styled garden – the only one of substance within the city walls.

Tourist office

☎ 0583 58 31 50

www.comune.lucca.it

Piazzale Verdi

☉ 9am-7pm summer, to 5.30pm winter

☑ Top Tips

▶ Be sure to walk along boutique-filled **Via Fillungo** and head into one of the side streets off its northeastern end to discover **Piazza Anfiteatro**, named after an amphitheatre that was located here in Roman times.

✖ Take a Break

▶ For picnic provisions, go to **Forno Amedeo Giusti** (Via Santa Lucia 20; pizzas & filled focaccias per kg €9-16; ☉7am-1pm & 4-7.30pm Mon-Sat, 4-7.30pm Sun) for focaccia or to **Da Felice** (www.pizzeriadafelice. com) for *cecina* (salted chickpea pizza) and *castagnacci* (chestnut cakes).

▶ Enjoy a coffee and slice of *buccellato* (Lucca's famous sweet bread loaf made with sultanas and aniseed seeds) at **Taddeucci** (www.taddeucci.com).

Explore

Siena

Unesco includes Siena's *centro storico* (historical centre) in its famed
World Heritage list, citing it as the living embodiment of a medieval
city. Easily explored in a day, the glories of its Gothic architecture
and art provide a fascinating contrast to the Renaissance splendor
that is so evident in Florence, making it a compelling side trip.

The Sights in a Day

☀ Upon arrival, make your way to the **Piazza del Campo** (p145) and join the locals knocking back their espressos at **Bar Il Palio** (p150). Next on the agenda should be the magnificent **Museo Civico** (p142), with its peerless collection of 14th-century secular art.

☼ Enjoy lunch at elegant **Enoteca I Terzi** (p147), popular with bankers from the headquarters of the nearby Banca Monte dei Paschi di Siena, the world's oldest bank. Afterwards, head to the **Opera della Metropolitana di Siena** (p138), visiting its *duomo* (cathedral), *battistero* (baptistry) and other attractions. At the end of your visit, pop over to the **Complesso Museale Santa Maria della Scala** (p145), on the opposite side of Piazza del Duomo, to see its famous *Pellegrinaio* (Pilgrim's Hall).

☾ Before heading back to Florence, enjoy a late-afternoon walk around the tranquil **Orto de' Pecci** (p145) or opt for a glass of Tuscan *vino* (wine) at **Enoteca Italiana** (p149) inside the Medici Fortress on the centre's eastern edge.

👁 Top Sights

Opera della Metropolitana di Siena (p138)

Museo Civico (p142)

🧡 Best of Florence

Eating

Enoteca I Terzi (p147)

Ristorante Grotta Santa Caterina da Bagoga (p147)

Tre Cristi (p148)

Grom (p150)

Kopa Kabana (p150)

Drinking

Caffè Fiorella (p149)

Enoteca I Terzi (p147)

Enoteca Italiana (p149)

Getting There

🚌 **Bus** Frequent 'Corse Rapide' (Express) buses leave from Florence's SITA Bus Station (€7.80, 1¼ hours). 'Corse Ordinarie' buses also run.

🚗 **Car** Take Florence–Siena S2 *superstrada* (expressway) or more scenic SR222. There are large car parks (€1.70 per hour) at San Francesco, Stadio Comunale, Fortezza Medicea and Santa Caterina (aka Fontebranda).

Top Sights
Opera della Metropolitana di Siena

Siena's *duomo* is one of Italy's greatest Gothic churches, and is also the focal point of an important group of ecclesiastical buildings that includes a museum, baptistry and crypt. All are embellished with wonderful art – Giovanni and Nicola Pisano, Bernardino Pinturicchio, Jacopo della Quercia, Lorenzo Ghiberti, Donatello and the most famous of all Sienese painters, Duccio di Buoninsegna, are only a few of the many talented artists who contributed works to glorify their city and their god.

◉ Map p144, B4

www.operaduomo.
siena.it

Piazza del Duomo

combined pass Mar-Oct
€12, Nov-Feb €8

⊙10.30am-6.30pm
Mon-Sat, 1.30-5.30pm
Sun Mar-Oct, to 5pm
Nov-Feb

Duomo ceiling, Siena

Don't Miss

Duomo

Construction of the **duomo** (Mar-Oct €4, Nov-Feb free) started in 1215 and work continued well into the 14th century. The magnificent facade of white, green and red marble was designed by Giovanni Pisano (the statues of philosophers and prophets are copies; you'll find the originals in the Museo dell'Opera). The interior is truly stunning, with walls and pillars continuing the black-and-white-stripe theme of the exterior.

Libreria Piccolomini

Through a door from the north aisle is this enchanting **library** (Piccolomini Library; included in duomo ticket Mar-Oct, €2 Nov-Feb), built to house the books of Enea Silvio Piccolomini, better known as Pius II. Its walls are decorated with vividly coloured narrative frescoes painted between 1502 and 1507 by Bernardino Pinturicchio depicting events in the life of Piccolomini, including his ordination as pope.

Pisano's Pulpit

The *duomo*'s exquisitely crafted marble and porphyry pulpit was created by Nicola Pisano, assisted by Arnolfo di Cambio, who later designed the *duomo* in Florence. Intricately carved with vigorous, realistic crowd scenes, it's one of the masterpieces of Gothic sculpture.

The Floor Panels

The inlaid-marble floor, decorated with 56 panels by about 40 artists and executed from the 14th to 16th centuries, depicts historical and biblical subjects. Unfortunately, about half of the panels are obscured by protective covering, and are revealed only between late-August and October each year (extra fee applies).

☑ Top Tips

▶ You'll save a lot of money (€12 to be exact) if you buy a combined OPA SI Pass, valid for three days, rather than individual tickets. It can be booked online. See the boxed text, p147 for details.

▶ Excellent guided one-hour tours of the *duomo* (11am, noon & 4pm daily; €5 plus entrance fee) are run by **Centro Guide Turistiche Siena e Provincia** (📞0577 4 32 73; info@guidesiena.it; Galleria Odeon, Via Banchi di Sopra 31; ⏰10am-1pm & 3-5pm Mon-Fri) between Easter and October. Tours (English and Italian) depart from the OPA SI ticket office; bookings advisable.

✗ Take a Break

▶ From the *battistero*, head towards Piazza Independenza; the city's most sophisticated lunch spot, Enoteca I Terzi, (p147) is nearby.

▶ On your way to enjoying Siena's best coffee at Caffè Fiorella (p149), stop at Panificio Il Magnifico (p150) to pick up some almond biscuits.

Battistero di San Giovanni

Behind the *duomo*, down a steep flight of steps, is the frescoed **baptistry** (Map p144; admission €4). At its centre is a hexagonal marble font by Jacopo della Quercia decorated with bronze panels depicting the life of St John the Baptist by artists including Lorenzo Ghiberti (*Baptism of Christ* and *St John in Prison*) and Donatello (*The Head of John the Baptist Being Presented to Herod*).

Cripta

This **crypt** (admission incl audioguide €6) below the cathedral's pulpit was rediscovered and restored in 1999 after having been filled to the roof with debris in the 1300s. The walls are completely covered with *pintura a secco* ('dry painting', better known as 'mural painting') dating back to the 1200s. There's some 180 sq m worth, depicting biblical stories including the Passion of Jesus and the Crucifixion.

Museo dell'Opera del Duomo

The collection at this **museum** (admission €7) showcases artworks that formerly adorned the *duomo*, including the 12 statues of prophets and philosophers by Giovanni Pisano that decorated its facade. Pisano designed these to be viewed from ground level, which is why they look so distorted as they crane uncomfortably forward. Also notable is the vibrant stained-glass window designed and painted by Duccio di Buoninsegna.

Duccio's Maestà

The highlight of the Museo dell'Opera del Duomo's collection is Duccio di Buoninsegna's striking *Maestà* (1311), which was painted on both sides as a screen for the *duomo*'s high altar. The main painting portrays the Virgin surrounded by angels, saints and prominent Sienese citizens of the period; the rear panels (sadly incomplete) portray scenes from the Passion of Christ.

Panorama del Facciatone

In 1339 the city's leaders decided to transform the cathedral into one of Italy's biggest churches, but the plague of 1348 scotched their plan to build an

Duomo, Siena

immense new nave with the present church as the transept. Known as the *Duomo Nuovo* (New Cathedral), all that remains of the project is this **panoramic terrace**, accessed through the museum.

Oratorio di San Bernardino

Nestled in the shadow of the huge Gothic church of San Francesco located northeast of the Campo is this 15th-century **oratory** (www.operaduomo. siena.it; Piazza San Francesco 9; adult/ reduced €3/2.50; ⏲1.30-6.30pm Mar-Oct), which is maintained by the Opera della Metropolitana di Siena (admission is included in the OPA SI Pass). The lower oratory has a star-studded blue vault and frescoes by Ventura Salimbeni, and the upstairs rooms contain works by Pietro Lorenzetti, Santi di Tito and Jacopo della Quercia.

Top Sights
Museo Civico

The city's most famous museum occupies rooms richly frescoed by artists of the Sienese school. These are unusual in that they were commissioned by the governing body of the city, rather than by the Church, and many depict secular subjects instead of the favoured religious themes of the time.

👁 Map p144, C4

www.comune.siena.it

Palazzo Comunale, Il Campo

adult/EU reduced €8/4.50

🕑10am-6.15pm mid-Mar–Oct, to 5.15pm Nov–mid-Mar

Detail of *Maestà* by Simone Martini, Museo Civico

Don't Miss

Entrance Rooms

The first room, the **Sala del Risorgimento**, is decorated with late-19th-century frescoes celebrating the life of the first king of Italy, Vittorio Emanuele II, and serialising key events in the Risorgimento (unification of Italy). Next to it is the **Sala di Balìa** (Room of Authority), with 15th-century frescoes recounting the life of Pope Alexander III (the Sienese Rolando Bandinelli).

Anticappella & Vestibolo

Taddeo di Bartolo painted the frescoes in the **Anticappella** (Chapel entrance hall) in 1415, illustrating the virtues needed for the proper exercise of power (Justice, Magnanimity, Strength, Prudence, Religion) as well as depictions of leading Republicans in ancient Rome. The **Vestibolo** (Vestibule) is next door; its star attraction is a bronze wolf, the symbol of Siena.

Simone Martini's Maestà

Simone Martini's striking *Maestà* (Virgin Mary in Majesty; 1315) holds court in the **Sala del Mappamondo** (Hall of the World Map); it is Martini's first known work. Another work attributed to Martini, his oft-reproduced fresco (1328–30) of Sienese army captain Guidoriccio da Fogliano, is opposite.

Allegories of Good and Bad Government

The **Sala dei Nove** (Hall of the Nine) showcases this splendid fresco cycle (c 1338–40) by Ambrogio Lorenzetti. The central allegory portrays scenes with personifications of Justice, Wisdom, Virtue and Peace. Set perpendicular from it are two scenes: one depicting an idyllic city with joyous citizens; the other filled with vice, crime and disease.

☑ Top Tips

▶ Four combined passes – SIA Summer, SIA Winter, Musei Comunali and Museo Civico/Torre del Mangia – cover the museum and can potentially save you money.

▶ After your visit, consider crossing the Campo and visiting the Museo delle Tavolette di Biccherna (p146), a modest but charming museum in the city's historic state archives.

✗ Take a Break

▶ Bar Il Palio (p150) on the Campo is a great coffee stop; stand at the bar for a quick coffee fix, or colonise a table to indulge in some peerless people-watching.

▶ One of Siena's best-loved restaurants, Osteria Le Logge (p149), is just around the corner.

N 0 —————————————— 200 m
0 —————————————— 0.1 miles

Viale dello Stadio

Viale Frederico Tozzi

Piazza Gramsci

Via dei Montanini

Via della Stufa Secca

Via di Vallerozzi

Piazza San Francesco

Stadio Comunale

La Lizza

Piazza Matteotti

Via Pianigiani

Piazza Salimbeni

Via dei Rossi

Via del Giglio

10 Vic di Provenzano

To Fortezza Medicea (500m)

Via del Paradiso

Via della Sapienza

Costa dell'Incrociata

Piazza Provenzano Salvani

15
21

Piazza San Domenico

Costa di Sant'Antonio

7

Via dei Termini

Via Banchi di Sopra

Piazza Tolomei

6 Chiesa di San Domenico

Via Camporegio

Casa Santuario di Santa Caterina

12

Via delle Terme

Via Cecco Angliolieri

Via Santa Caterina

Via della Galluza

9

8

Piazza Indipendenza

Banchi di Sotto

16 Museo delle Tavolette di Biccherna

Vic delle Scotte

5

13

Via di Pantanet

Via di Fontebranda

19

Battistero di San Giovanni & Cripta

14

Via del Porrione

Piazza del Campo 1

Palazzo Comunale

Via dei Pellegrini

Piazza San Giovanni

17

Museo dell'Opera del Duomo & Panorama del Facciatone

Museo Civico 2

Opera della Metropolitana di Siena

Duomo

Piazza Jacopo della Quercia

Via di Salicotto

Piazza di Selva

4

Complesso Museale Santa Maria della Scala

Via del Capitano

Piazza del Duomo

Via del Castoro

Piazza del Mercato

Via Giovanni Duprè

Via del Sole

20

Via di Città

Via del Casato di Sotto

Casato di Sopra

Via S. Agata

Piazza di Postierla

Via San Pietro

Orto de' Pecci

Piazza delle Due Porte

Via di Stalloreggi

3 Pinacoteca Nazionale

18

Sights

Piazza del Campo
PIAZZA

1 ⊙ Map p144, C3

This sloping piazza, popularly known as Il Campo, has been Siena's civic and social centre since its creation in the mid-12th century. Its pie-piece paving design is divided into nine sectors and its **Fonte Gaia** (Happy Fountain) dates from 1346. These days the fountain's carved panels are reproductions (the originals are on display in the Complesso Museale Santa Maria della Scala).

Palazzo Comunale
HISTORIC BUILDING

2 ⊙ Map p144, D4

At the lowest point of the Campo stands this graceful Gothic building, purpose-built in the late 13th century as the piazza's centrepiece. Entry to its ground-floor central courtyard is free, and from it soars the graceful **Torre del Mangia** (⊙10am-6.15pm Mar–mid-Oct, to 3.15pm mid-Oct–Feb; admission €8), 102m high and with 500-odd steps. The views from the top are magnificent. (Palazzo Pubblico)

Pinacoteca Nazionale
ART GALLERY

3 ⊙ Map p144, C5

Occupying the once-grand but now sadly disheveled 14th-century Palazzo Buonsignori, this labyrinthine gallery displays an extraordinary collection of Gothic masterpieces from the Sienese

Q Local Life

Orto de' Pecci

Head down the hill past Piazza del Mercato to discover the urban oasis of **Orto de' Pecci** (Map p144, D5; www.ortodepecci.it; admission free; ⊙24hr). Kids love visiting the geese, goats, ducks and donkeys that live here, and locals can often be found hiding from the tourist masses in its green spaces (perfect for picnics or an afternoon snooze). There's a medieval garden, an experimental vineyard which Siena University's agriculture department has planted with clones of medieval vines, and a cooperative organic farm that grows fruit and vegetables and supplies an on-site **restaurant** (⊙12.30-2.30pm & 7.30-10pm Tue-Sat, to 2.30pm Sun Mar-Oct, to 2.30pm & 7.30-10pm Fri & Sat, to 2.30pm Sun Nov-Feb) with produce.

school. The highlights are all on the 2nd floor, including magnificent and uplifting works by Duccio di Buoninsegna, Simone Martini, Niccolò di Segna, Lippo Memmi, Ambrogio and Pietro Lorenzetti, Bartolo di Fredi and Taddeo di Bartolo. (Via San Pietro 29; adult/reduced €4/2; ⊙10am-5.45pm Tue-Sat, 9am-12.45pm Sun & Mon)

Complesso Museale Santa Maria della Scala
CULTURAL BUILDING

4 ⊙ Map p144, B4

This former hospital, parts of which date to the 13th century, was built as a hospice for pilgrims travelling the Via Francigena from Canterbury to Rome. Located opposite the *duomo,* its highlight is the upstairs Pellegrinaio (Pilgrim's Hall), with vivid 15th-century frescoes by Lorenzo Vecchietta, Priamo della Quercia and Domenico di Bartolo lauding the good works of the hospital and its patrons. (www.santamariadellascala.com; Piazza del Duomo 1; adult/reduced/child under 11 €6/3.50/free; 10.30am-4pm, to 6.30pm in high season)

Museo delle Tavolette di Biccherna
MUSEUM

5 Map p144, D3

Siena's state archives are housed in the Renaissance-era **Palazzo Piccolomini**, close to the Campo. Enter from the courtyard and take the elevator to the 4th floor to visit this charming museum, which takes its name from the pride of its collection, a series of small, late-13th-century paintings known as the '*Tavolette di Biccherna*'. Guided tours (Italian only) are compulsory. (archiviostato.si.it, in Italian; Banchi di Sotto 52; admission free; guided tours 9.30am, 10.30am & 11.30am Mon-Sat)

Chiesa di San Domenico
CHURCH

6 Map p144, A2

St Catherine was welcomed into the Dominican fold within this imposing church, and its **Cappella di Santa Caterina** is adorned with frescoes by Il Sodoma depicting events in her life. Catherine died in Rome, where most of her body is preserved, but her head was returned to Siena (it's in a 15th-

Understand
The Palio
--- --- --- --- --- --- --- --- --- ---

Dating from the Middle Ages, this spectacular annual event includes a series of colourful pageants and a wild horse race on 2 July and 16 August in which 10 of Siena's 17 *contrade* (town districts) compete for the coveted *palio* (silk banner).

The race is staged in the Campo. From about 5pm, representatives from each *contrada* parade in historical costume, all bearing their individual banners. For scarcely one exhilarating minute, the 10 horses and their bareback riders tear three times around a temporarily constructed dirt racetrack with a speed and violence that makes spectators' hair stand on end.

The race is held at 7.45pm in July and 7pm in August. Join the crowds in the centre of the Campo at least four hours before the start if you want a place on the rails. Alternatively, cafes in the Campo sell expensive places on their terraces; these can be booked through the **tourist office** (0577 28 05 51; www.terresiena.it; Piazza del Campo 56; 9.30am-6.30pm Easter-Sep, to 5.30pm Mon-Fri, to 12.30pm Sun Oct-Easter) up to one year in advance.

century tabernacle above the altar in the chapel). (Piazza San Domenico; ⊘9am-12.30pm & 3-7pm)

Casa Santuario di Santa Caterina
RELIGIOUS

7 ◉ Map p144, B2

If you want more of Santa Caterina – figuratively speaking – visit this pilgrimage sight where the saint, her parents and 24 siblings lived (locals like to joke that her mother must have been a saint, too). The rooms in the house were converted into small chapels in the 15th century. (Costa di Sant'Antonio 6; admission free; ⊘9am-6.30pm Mar-Nov, 10am-6pm Dec-Feb)

Eating

Enoteca I Terzi
MODERN TUSCAN €€

8 ✕ Map p144, C3

Close to the Campo but off the well-beaten tourist trail, this classy, modern *enoteca* (wine bar) is a favourite with sophisticated locals, who linger over working lunches, *aperitivi* (pre-dinner drinks accompanied by cocktail snacks) sessions and casual dinners featuring top-notch *salumi* (cured meats), delicate handmade pasta, flavoursome risotto and succulent grilled meats. The wine list is fantastic, and includes an excellent choice by the glass. Go. (☎0577 4 43 29; www.enotecaiterzi.it; Via dei Termini 7; antipasto plate €9, meals €35; ⊘11am-1am Mon-Sat)

Top Tip
Combined Passes

In addition to the OPA SI Pass (p137), consider these money-saving combined passes (purchase directly at museums):

▶ **SIA Summer** (Museo Civico, Complesso Museale Santa Maria della Scala, Museo dell'Opera, Battistero di San Giovanni, Oratorio di San Bernardino and Chiesa di San Agostino; €17, valid for seven days during period 15 March to 31 October)

▶ **SIA Winter** (Museo Civico, Complesso Museale Santa Maria della Scala, Museo dell'Opera and Battistero di San Giovanni; €14, valid for seven days during period 1 November to 14 March)

▶ **Museo Civico/Torre del Mangia** (€13)

▶ **Musei Comunali** (Museo Civico and Complesso Museale Santa Maria della Scala; €11, valid for two days)

Ristorante Grotta Santa Caterina da Bagoga
TUSCAN €€

9 ✕ Map p144, B3

Pierino Fagnani ('Bagogoga'), one of Siena's most famous *palio* (silk banner) jockeys, swapped his saddle for an apron in 1973 and has been operating this much-loved restaurant near the Casa Santuario di Santa Caterina ever since. Traditional Tuscan palate

Osteria Le Logge

pleasers feature on the menu, and are perhaps best appreciated in the four-course *'tipico'* (€35) or *'degustazione'* (€50 with wine) menus. (📞0577 28 22 08; www.bagoga.it; Via della Galluzza 26; meals €28; ⏱12.30-2.30pm & 7.30-10.30pm Tue-Sat, to 2.30pm Sun)

Tre Cristi
SEAFOOD €€€

10 🍴 Map p144, D1

Seafood restaurants are thin on the ground in this meat-obsessed region, so the long existence of Tre Cristi (it's been around since 1830) should be heartily celebrated. The menu here is as elegant as the decor, and added touches such as a complimentary glass of *prosecco* (dry sparkling wine) at the start of the meal add to the experience. (📞0577 28 06 08; www.trecristi.com; Vicolo di Provenzano 1; 3-course tasting menus €35-45, 5-course menus €65; ⏱12.30-3pm & 7.30-10.30pm Mon-Sat)

Morbidi
DELI €

11 🍴 Map p144, C2

Local gastronomes shop here as the range of cheese, cured meats and imported delicacies is the best in Siena. Also notable is the downstairs lunch buffet, which offers fantastic value. For a mere €12, you can graze on platters of antipasti, salads, pastas and a dessert of the day. Bottled water is

supplied, wine and coffee cost extra.
(www.morbidi.com; Via Banchi di Sopra 75;
buffet €12; ⏱9am-8pm Mon-Sat, lunch buffet
12.30-2.30pm)

La Compagnia dei Vinattieri

WINE BAR €€

12 🍴 Map p144, C2

Duck down the stairs to enjoy a quick
glass of wine and a meat or cheese
platter in this cellar, or settle in for a
leisurely meal accompanied by your
choice from an impressive wine list.
It's popular with locals and tourists
alike – you'll need to try your luck for a
drink, and book in advance for a meal.
(📞0577 23 65 68; www.vinattieri.net; Via delle
Terme 79; antipasto platter €7-9, meals €35;
⏱noon-10pm, closed late Feb–late Mar)

Osteria Le Logge

MODERN TUSCAN €€€

13 🍴 Map p144, D3

This place changes its menu of creative Tuscan cuisine almost daily. The
best tables are in the downstairs
dining room – once a pharmacy and
still retaining its handsome display
cabinets – or on the streetside terrace.
We've found that the antipasti and
primi (first courses) are consist-
ently delicious, but the mains can be
disappointing. (📞0577 4 80 13; www.
osterialelogge.it; Via del Porrione 33; meals
€55; ⏱noon-2.45 & 7-10.30pm Mon-Sat)

◯ Local Life
Consorzio Agrario di Siena
Operating since 1901, this **farmer's
co-op** (Map p144, B2; Via Pianigiani
13; ⏱8am-7.30pm Mon-Sat) is a rich
emporium of food and wine, much
of it locally produced, and is an
essential stop for self-caterers.
There's also a small bar area where
locals flock to purchase and eat
slabs of freshly cooked pizza (€12
to €14.30 per kilogram).

Drinking

Caffè Fiorella

CAFE

14 🍺 Map p144, C3

Squeeze into this tiny space behind
the Campo to enjoy Siena's best coffee. In summer, the coffee granita
with a dollop of cream is a wonderful
indulgence. (www.torrefazionefiorella.it; Via
di Città 13; ⏱7am-8pm Mon-Sat)

Enoteca Italiana

WINE BAR

15 🍺 Map p144, A2

The former munitions cellar and
dungeon of this Medici fortress has
been artfully transformed into a
classy *enoteca* that carries over 1500
Italian labels. You can take a bottle
with you, ship a case home or enjoy
a drop in the attractive courtyard or
atmospheric

Local Life
Gelati Stops

Conveniently close to the Campo and usually host to a long queue, **Grom** (Map p144, C3; www.grom.it; Via Banchi di Sopra 11-13; gelato €2.50-5.50; ⏲11am-midnight Sun-Thu, to 12.30am Fri & Sat Apr-Sep, 11am-11pm Sun-Thu, to midnight Fri & Sat Oct-Mar) serves delectable gelato with flavours that change with the season; many of the ingredients are organic or Slow Food–accredited. On the route to Piazza San Francesco is home-grown favourite, **Kopa Kabana** (Map p144, C2; www.gelateriakopa-kabana.it; Via dei Rossi 52-55; gelati €1.80-4.30; ⏲noon-8pm mid-Feb–mid-Nov, later hr in warm weather), where the icy concoctions are feshly made by self-proclaimed ice-cream master, Fabio (we're pleased to concur). Both are hugely popular with Sienese of all ages.

vaulted interior of the wine bar. There's often food available, too. (www.enoteca-italiana.it; Fortezza Medicea; ⏲noon-1am Mon-Sat Apr-Sep, to midnight Oct-Mar)

Bar II Palio   CAFE

16 🍴 Map p144, C3

The best coffee on the Campo; drink it standing at the bar or suffer the financial consequences. (Piazza del Campo 47; ⏲8am-midnight)

Shopping

Panificio II Magnifico   FOOD

17 🔒 Map p144, C3

Lorenzo Rossi is Siena's best baker, and his *panforte* (rich and chewy cake made with almonds, honey and candied fruit), *ricciarelli* (sugar-dusted chewy almond biscuits) and *cavallucci* (almond biscuits made with Tuscan millefiori honey) are a weekly purchase for most local households. (www.ilmagnifico.siena.it; Via dei Pellegrini 27; ⏲7.30am-7.30pm Mon-Sat)

Bottega d'Arte   ART

18 🔒 Map p144, B5

Inspired by the works of Sienese masters of the 14th and 15th centuries, artists Chiara Perinetti Casoni and Michelangelo Attardo Perinetti Casoni create exquisite icons in tempera and 24-carat gold leaf. Expensive? Yes. Worth it? You bet. (www.arteinsiena.it; Via Stalloreggi 47)

Il Pellicano   CERAMICS

19 🔒 Map p144, B3

Elisabetta Ricci has been making traditional hand-painted Sienese ceramics for over 30 years. She shapes, fires and paints her ceramic creations – often using Renaissance-era styles or typical *contrade* (district) designs – at her atelier near Parking Santa Caterina and sells them at this

Pizzicheria de Miccoli

shop near the *duomo*. Elisabetta also conducts lessons in traditional ceramic techniques – contact her for details. (📞0577 24 79 14; www.siena-ilpellicano.it; Via Diacceto 17a; ⏱10.30am-7pm Easter-Oct, 10.30am-7pm Mon-Sat Nov-Easter)

Pizzicheria de Miccoli   FOOD

20 🅟 Map p144, C4

Richly scented, de Miccoli has a stuffed boar's head over its entrance and windows festooned with sausages, stacks of cheese and sacks of porcini mushrooms. It also sells filled *panini*

(sandwiches) to go. (Via di Città 93-95; ⏱8am-8pm)

Wednesday Market   MARKET

21 🅟 Map p144, A2

Spreading around Fortezza Medicea (Medici fortress) and towards the Stadio Comunale (city sports stadium), this is one of Tuscany's largest markets and is great for foodstuffs and cheap clothing. An antiques market is also held here on the third Sunday of each month. (⏱7.30am-1pm)

Top Sights
Chianti

Getting There

🚗 Take the SR222
(Via Chiantigiana)

Split between the provinces of Florence (Chianti Fiorentino) and Siena (Chianti Senese), this photogenic wine region is criss-crossed by a picturesque network of *strade provinciale* (provincial roads) and *strade secondaria* (secondary roads), some of which are unsealed. An easy drive from Florence, you'll see immaculately maintained vineyards and olive groves, honey-coloured stone farmhouses, dense forests, graceful Romanesque *pieve* (rural churches), handsome Renaissance villas and imposing stone castles built by Florentine and Sienese warlords during the Middle Ages.

Vineyards, Chianti

Don't Miss

Badia a Passignano

This 11th-century abbey is surrounded by a picturesque **wine estate** (www.osteriadipassignano.com) owned by the Antinoris, one of Tuscany's best known winemaking families. The vineyards and historic cellars can be visited by guided tour, you can taste wines in the *cantina* (cellar) and there's a highly regarded restaurant.

Antinori nel Chianti Classico

To reach this recently opened **cellar complex** (www.antinorichianticlassico.it; Via Cassia per Siena 133, Località Bargino; tour & tasting €20, bookings essential; ⊙11am-6pm Mon-Sat, to 2pm Sun), pass through a security check to reach the main building, built into the hillside. One-hour guided tours finish with a tasting of three Antinori wines in an all-glass room suspended above barrels in the cellar (wow!).

Castello di Brolio

Home to the aristocratic Ricasoli family, this 11th-century **wine estate** (☑0577 73 02 80; www.ricasoli.it; self-guided tour of garden, chapel & crypt €5, guided tour of museum, chapel & crypt €8; ⊙10am-5.30pm mid-Mar–Nov, guided tours every 30 minutes 10am-1pm & 2.30-5.30pm Tue-Sun) is the oldest in Italy. It opens its formal garden, panoramic terrace and small museum to day-trippers, along with an *osteria* (casual tavern) and a *cantina*.

Castello di Ama

In recent years this highly regarded **wine estate** (☑0577 74 60 31; http://arte.castellodiama.com; guided tours €15, with wine & oil tasting €35; ⊙year round, by appt) near Gaiole in Chianti has developed a sculpture park showcasing 13 site-specific artworks by major international artists.

Tourist office

☑055 854 62 99

info@turismo.grev einchianti.eu

Piazza Matteotti 11, Greve in Chianti

⊙10am-7pm

☑ Top Tips

▶ *Le strade del Gallo Nero* (€2.50) is a useful map of the wine-producing zone showing both major and secondary roads and including a comprehensive list of wine estates. It's available at newsstands throughout Chianti.

▶ Advance bookings are essential to visit Antinori nel Chianti Classico, Castello di Ama and the vineyards and cellar at Badia a Passignano.

✕ Take a Break

▶ Head to the picturesque hilltop village of **Volpaia** near Radda in Chianti to visit the *cantina* of the Castello di Volpaia wine estate, enjoy a snack at **Bar Ucci** (www.bar-ucci.it) or lunch at **Ristorante La Bottega** (☑0577 73 80 01; www.labottegadivol paia.it).

Top Sights
San Gimignano

Getting There

🚌 To/from Florence (€6.80, 1¼ to two hours, 10 daily Mon-Sat). Note: possible change at Poggibonsi.

🚗 Siena–Florence superstrada, SR2 and SP1. Park at Parcheggio Montemaggio (per hour/24 hours €2/20).

As you crest the hill coming from the east, the 15 towers of this walled hilltop town look like a medieval Manhattan. Originally an Etruscan village, San Gimignano grew and became prosperous in the Middle Ages due to its location on the Via Francigena pilgrimage route. Sadly, many of its inhabitants died in the 1348 plague. Today, not even the plague would deter the swarms of summer day-trippers lured by the town's intact medieval streetscapes and enchanting rural setting.

Towers, San Gimignano

Don't Miss

Collegiata

San Gimignano's Romanesque cathedral is known as the **Collegiata** (Piazza del Duomo; ⏱10am-7.10pm Mon-Fri, to 5.10pm Sat, 12.30-7.10pm Sun Apr-Oct, shorter hr rest of year, closed 2nd half Nov & Jan; adult/child €3.50/1.50), a reference to the college of priests who originally managed it. Parts of the building date back to the second half of the 11th century, but its remarkably vivid frescoes, which resemble a vast medieval comic strip, date from the 14th century.

Museo Civico

Housed in the 12th-century Palazzo Civico (Town Hall), this **museum** (Piazza del Duomo; ⏱9.30am-7pm Apr-Sep, 11am-5.30pm Oct-Mar; adult/child €5/4) is built around the handsome **Sala di Dante**, where the great poet once met with the town's dignitaries. The adjoining **Pinacoteca** (Art Gallery) has paintings from the Sienese and Florentine schools of the 12th to 15th centuries.

Torre Grossa

While at the Museo Civico, be sure to climb the 154 steps to reach the top of this **tower** (the only one of the town's towers accessible to the public). The views are spectacular.

Museo del Vino

Housed in an unmarked gallery next to the *rocca* (fortress), this tiny **museum** (Wine Museum; museo delvino@sangimignano.com; Parco della Rocca; admission free; ⏱11.30am-6.30pm Apr-Oct) celebrates Vernaccia, San Gimignano's famous wine. It comprises a small exhibition (in Italian) on the history of the varietal and an *enoteca* (wine bar) where you can purchase a glass of wine to enjoy on the terrace, which has a panoramic view.

Tourist office

☎0577 94 00 08

www.sangimignano.com

Piazza del Duomo 1

⏱10am-1pm & 3-7pm Mar-Oct, 10am-1pm & 2-6pm Nov-Feb

☑ Top Tips

▶ The extremely helpful tourist office (p155) supplies maps and organises tours.

▶ Free wi-fi is available in and around Piazza del Duomo.

▶ Be sure to sample local white wine Vernaccia di San Gimignano.

✕ Take a Break

▶ Try the pasta dishes and excellent house Vernaccia at **Ristorante La Mandragola** (☎0577 94 03 77; www.locanda lamandragola.it).

▶ Grab a *panino* (sandwich) with locally sourced ingredients at **Dal Bertelli** (Via Capassi 30; panini €3-5, glasses of wine €1.50; ⏱1-7pm Mar-early Jan) and a sweet finale at **Gelateria Dondoli** (www.gelateria-dipiazza.com).

The Best of
Florence & Tuscany

Gelato display in a Florence store
LISA J. GOODMAN/GETTY IMAGES ©

Best Walks
Heart of the City

Every visitor to Florence spends time navigating the cobbled medieval lanes that run between Via de' Tornabuoni and Via del Proconsolo but few explore them thoroughly, instead focusing on the major monuments and spaces. This walk will introduce you to some less visited sights and laneways.

🏃 The Walk

Start Piazza della Repubblica

Finish La Terrazza bar

Length 2km; two hours

✗ Take a Break

Fashionable Via de' Tornabuoni is the heart of Florence's cafe society. **Procacci** (p45), **Caffè Giacosa** (p58) and **Le Renaissance Café** (p45) are great choices.

Columns, Piazza della Repubblica (p40)

PAUL EDMONDSON/GETTY IMAGES ©

❶ Piazza della Repubblica

Start with a coffee at one of the historic cafes on this handsome 19th-century **square** (p40). Its construction entailed the demolition of a Jewish ghetto and produce market, and the relocation of nearly 6000 residents.

❷ Chiesa e Museo di Orsanmichele

Take Via Calimala then Via Orsanmichele to reach this unique **church** (p38), created in the 14th century when the arcades of a century-old grain market were walled in and two storeys added.

❸ Mercato Nuovo

Back at Via Calimala, continue walking south until you see the 16th-century **'New Market'** (p47). Florentines call the bronze statue of a wild boar on its southern side 'Il Porcellino' (The Piglet) – rub its snout to ensure your return to Florence!

❹ Museo di Palazzo Davanzati

On Via Porta Rossa is this 14th-century **ware-**

house residence (p39) with its studded doors and central loggia. A few doors down, next to the Slowly bar, peep through the sturdy iron gate and up to see the ancient brick vaults.

⑤ Chiesa di Santa Trinìta

Continue to Via de' Tornabuoni, the city's most famous shopping strip. Cross Piazza Santa Trinìta, looking up to admire 13th-century Palazzo Spini-Feroni, home of Salvatore Ferragamo's flagship store.

Then enter this **church** (p54) to admire its frescoed chapels.

⑥ Via del Parione

Wander down this narrow street filled with old mansions (now apartments) and artisan's workshops. Pop into paper marbler **Alberto Cozzi** (p61) and puppet maker **Letizia Fiorini** (p58) to see them at work.

⑦ Chiesa dei Santissimi Apostoli

Back to Via de' Tornabuoni, veer into Borgo

SS Apostoli for this Romanesque **church** set in a sunken square once used as a cemetery for unbaptised babies. Onwards, find Tuscan olive-oil products in **La Bottega dell'Olio** (p46) and resin jewellery at **Angela Caputi** (p46).

⑧ Hotel Continental

Continue around to the Hotel Continental. Finish your walk at its **rooftop bar** (p44), which has a spectacular view of the Ponte Vecchio.

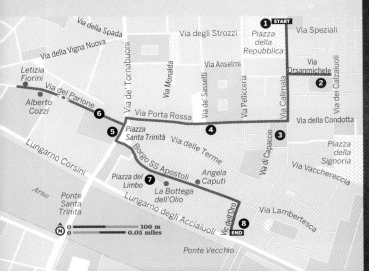

Best Walks
A Renaissance Tour

This greatest-hits tour crams a huge amount of culture into a very tight timeline – you'll need to proceed at a cracking pace to see everything in four hours. Alternatively – and preferably – divide it over two days to ensure that you do all of the sights justice.

🏃 The Walk

Start Cappelle Medicee

Finish Basilica di Santa Croce

Length 3.2km; at least four hours

🍴 Take a Break

Piazza della Signoria is a hugely atmospheric spot for a coffee or drink. Popular pitstops include **Caffè Rivoire** (p45) and **Gucci Museo Caffè** (p45).

Piazza della Signoria (p39)

❶ Cappelle Medicee

Start in the territory of Renaissance powerbrokers and art patrons, the Medicis, who commissioned a number of self-aggrandising monuments on San Lorenzo's streets. The greatest is this **mausoleum** (p70), partly designed by Michelangelo; it contains three of his most magnificent sculptures.

❷ Palazzo Medici-Ricciardi

Duck through the market stalls on Piazza San Lorenzo to reach this Medici **palace** (p71), commissioned by Cosimo the Elder and designed by Michelozzo. After admiring the facade, head inside to see Benozzo Gozzoli's vivid frescoes in the Cappella dei Magi. Afterwards, enjoy a traditional Tuscan meal at **Trattoria Mario** (p73).

❸ Galleria dell'Accademia

It's time to see the work of art most synonymous with the Renaissance – Michelangelo's statue of David in the

Accademia (p64). A powerful evocation of the Humanist principles that underpinned this period, you'll find that it more than lives up to its huge reputation.

④ Ospedale degli Innocenti

Next, make your way to the Brunelleschi-designed loggia on this **orphanage** (p72), which architectural historians credit as one of the great triumphs of Renaissance architecture. While here, soak up the local atmosphere in the piazza.

⑤ Duomo

Head to the **duomo** (p24), and climb to the top of its dome – another Brunelleschi masterpiece – to enjoy a 360-degree panorama over the city.

⑥ Piazza della Signoria

Head south down Via del Proconsolo and then west to wander through the city's most spectacular **piazza** (p39), viewing the sculptures under the Loggia dei Lanzi and noting the location of the Uffizi – repository of the world's

pre-eminent collection of Renaissance art – for future visits.

⑦ Basilica di Santa Croce

Follow pedestrianised Borgo dei Greci to reach your final stop, the huge Franciscan **basilica** (p86) where Renaissance luminaries including Michelangelo, Machiavelli, Galileo and Ghiberti are buried. Ogle Giotto frescoes in the Cappella Bardi and admire Brunelleschi's exquisite Cappella de' Pazzi.

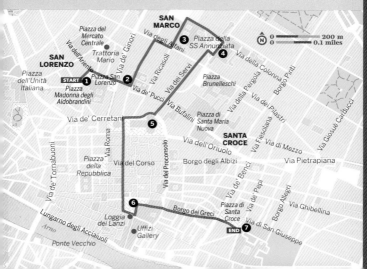

Best
Shopping

In medieval and Renaissance Florence, goldsmiths, silversmiths and shoemakers were as highly regarded as sculptors and artists. Today, Florentines are equally enamoured of design and artisanship and go out of their way to source quality goods. Most are also happy to pay what's required (usually a considerable amount) to *fare la bella figura* (cut a fine figure).

Fashion

Florentines take great pride in their dress and appearance, which is not surprising given that the Italian fashion industry was born here. Guccio Gucci and Salvatore Farragamo got the haute-couture ball rolling in the 1920s, and the first Italian prêt-à-porter show was staged here in 1951.

Via de'Tornabuoni and its surrounding streets – especially Via della Vigna Nuova, Via della Spada and Borgo SS Apostoli – are the city's fashion epicentre, home to upmarket designers from Italy and abroad. Some up-and-coming designers are also here, although high rents mean that they are more likely to be located in the Oltrano and Santa Croce.

Artisanal Crafts

Cheap imported handbags and other goods are common, especially in the city's two main markets, Mercato Centrale and Mercato Nuovo. But for serious shoppers keen to delve into a city synonymous with craftsmanship, there are plenty of traditional boutiques and *botteghe* (workshops) to visit. Many of these are in the neighbourhood of Oltrano, south of the Arno; see p114 for details.

Traditional artisan wares produced by hand or on centuries-old machinery include jewellery, leathergoods (shoes, gloves, bags), fabrics and stationery including marbled paper and bound journals.

GIORGIO COSULICH/GETTY IMAGES ©

Best Artisan Crafts

Letizia Fiorini Handmade traditional Italian puppets (p58)

Antico Setifico Fiorentino Opulent damasks and brocades (p115)

Scarpelli Mosaici Specialises in *pietre dure* (puzzle-like marble mosaics; p78)

Best Leather

Francesco da Firenze Hand-stitched men's and women's leather shoes (p115)

Casini Firenze Beautifully crafted clothes, bags and shoes (p115)

Madova Gloves in every colour and style (p114)

Best Jewellery

Angela Caputi Bold and colourful resin jewellery (p46)

Shopping, Via de' Tornabuoni (p46)

Alessandro Dari Sculptural, hand-made pieces (p111)

Mio Concept Stylish design objects (p59)

Best Fashion

A Piedi Nudi nel Parco Stocks super-chic avant-garde designers (p47)

Alessandro Gherardeschi Distinctive men's and women's shirts and blouses (p61)

Loretta Caponi Gorgeous, hand-embroidered sleepwear, bed and table linen (p61)

Grevi Hats for every occasion (p60)

Best Paper Products

Giulio Giannini e Figlio Making marbled paper, beautifully bound books and stationery since 1856 (p115)

Pineider Selling paper products and elegant leather office accessories since 1774 (pictured left; p46)

Alberto Cozzi Marbled paper, leather-bound journals and colourful cards (p61)

Best Perfume & Soap

Officina Profumo-Farmaceutica di Santa Maria Novella Perfumery-pharmacy established in 1612 (p61)

Lorenzo Villoresi Bespoke perfumes and potpourris (p111)

La Bottega dell'Olio Oils, soaps and skincare products made with olive oil (p46)

Best Foodstuffs

Dolce Forte Hand-made chocolates (p59)

Worth a Trip

Designer outlets:
Barberino Designer Outlet (www.mcarthurglen.it; Via Meucci, Barberino di Mugello; ⏰10am-8pm Mon-Fri, to 9pm Sat & Sun) 40km north of Florence; buses (adult/reduced return €15/8, 35 minutes, 10am and 2.30pm) from Piazza della Stazione.
The Mall (www.themall.it; Via Europa 8, Leccio; ⏰10am-7pm) 30km southeast of Florence; buses (€5) from SITA bus station between 8.50am and 1pm, returns between 2pm and 6.30pm.

Panificio Il Magnifico Traditional Sienese biscuits (p150)

Best
Architecture

Three architectural styles are showcased in Florence: Romanesque, Tuscan Gothic and Renaissance. The latter originated here – before taking the rest of Italy and Europe by storm – and is the city's emblematic style.

MARK BOLTON/GETTY IMAGES ©

Romanesque Architecture

A blow-in from Northern Europe, the Romanesque style was given a unique local twist in Tuscany, where church facades were given alternating stripes of green and white marble. Generally, Romanesque buildings displayed an emphasis on width and the horizontal lines of a building rather than height, and featured church groups with campaniles and baptistries that were separate to the church.

Gothic Architecture

The Tuscans didn't embrace the Gothic as enthusiastically as their northern neighbours; the flying buttresses, grotesque gargoyles and over-the-top decoration were just too far from the classical ideal that was (and still is) bred in the Tuscan bone. There were, of course, exceptions; most notably the *duomo* (cathedral) in Siena.

Renaissance Architecture

When the dome of Florence's *duomo* was completed in 1436, Leon Battista Alberti called it the first great achievement of the 'new' architecture, one that equalled or even surpassed the great buildings of antiquity. The elegance of line, innovation in building method and references to antiquity that characterised Brunelleschi's work were emulated by other Florentine architects, leading to this pared-down, classically inspired style dominating local architecture throughout the 15th and 16th centuries.

☑ **Top Tips**

▶ Guided walking tours of the city are a great way to learn about and appreciate its architecture. Recommended operators include **Freya's Florence** (☎ 349 074 89 07; www.freyasflorence. com; per hr €70) and **ArtViva** (☎ 055 264 50 33; www.italy.artviva. com; Via de' Sassetti 1; per person from €25).

Best Romanesque Architecture

Basilica di San Miniato al Monte Built in the 11th century, with a fine crypt (p108)

Basilica Santa Maria Novella Transitional from Romanesque to Gothic (p50)

Basilica di Santa Croce (p86)

Battistero di San Giovanni Octagonal structure with striking green-and-white marble exterior (p140)

Piazza dei Miracoli, Pisa Peerless example of a Romanesque cathedral group (p126)

Cattedrale di San Martino, Lucca Unusual Romanesque facade and rebuilt Gothic interior (p135)

Best Tuscan Gothic Architecture

Duomo, Siena Polychrome marble facade and black-and-white striped interior (p138)

Duomo Exquisite facade and elegant *campanile* (bell tower; p24)

Palazzo Comunale, Siena Ingeniously designed concave facade complementing the convex curve of Piazza del Campo (p145)

Chiesa di Santa Maria della Spina, Pisa Ornately decorated exterior (p131)

Best Renaissance Architecture

Duomo Brunelleschi's dome is considered the finest and most influential achievement of Renaissance architecture (p24)

Ospedale degli Innocenti Classically elegant loggia (p72)

Cappella de' Pazzi, Basilica di Santa Croce Sublimely beautiful exercise in architectural harmony (p86)

Biblioteca Medicea Laurenziana Michelangelo's staircase pre-empts Baroque curves (p71)

Basilica di San Lorenzo Harmonious design with a particularly beautiful sacristy (p66)

Cappelle Medicee Sumptuous Michelangelo design where no cost was spared (p70)

Palazzo Pitti Muscular design that shouts power and prestige (p100)

Palazzo Medici-Ricciardi The prototype of Renaissance civic architecture (p71)

Palazzo Strozzi The last and most magnificent of the palaces built in the Renaissance (p38)

Best
Views

Best Views from Monuments

Campanile & Dome, Duomo 360 degree views over the historic centre (p24)

Uffizi Gallery Snapshot of riverside Florence from the *Secondo Corridoio* (Second Corridor; p30)

Palazzo Vecchio Bird's-eye view of the historic centre from the battlements of the Torre d'Arnolfo (p34)

Leaning Tower, Pisa Over the Piazza dei Miracoli and city towards the Apuane Alps (p127)

Torre del Mangia, Siena Vertiginous viewpoint from which to watch action in the Campo (pictured; p145)

Torre Grossa, San Gimignano Glorious views over the countryside (p155)

Panorama del Facciatone, Siena Over the terracotta-coloured rooftops of the historical centre (p138)

Basilica di San Miniato al Monte Elevated location with a terrace overlooking the city skyline (p108)

Best Views from Gardens & Parks

Giardino di Boboli Look back onto the Palazzo Pitti or over gentle slopes of olive trees (p104)

Giardino Bardini Take tea on the loggia while savouring a view of the city skyline (p105)

Best View from Public Spaces

Piazzale Michelangelo See Florence unfurled from the city's most spectacular vantage point (p105)

Basilica di Sant'Alessandro, Fiesole Intoxicating view over Florence from the terrace next to the church (p81)

Ponte Vecchio The most romantic sunset view in Florence; enjoy it from the central belvederes (p118)

Ponte Santa Trìnita Enjoy a DIY *aperitivo* (pre-dinner drinks with

VISIONS OF OUR LAND/GETTY IMAGES ©

cocktail snacks) and Arno views under the bridge (p54)

Best Restaurant & Bar Views

La Reggia degli Etruschi, Fiesole Stupendous views over Florence from the dining room and terrace (p81)

Open Bar Sip cocktails while watching the Arno swirl beneath your feet (p110)

Caffè Rivoire Box-seat view of picturesque Piazza della Signoria (p160)

Villa Aurora, Fiesole Fabulous Florentine panorama from the historic, pagoda-covered lunch terrace (p81)

La Terrazza Chic setting in which to watch the sun set over the Arno (p44)

Best
Nightlife

Let's be frank: Florence is many wonderful things, but it's not a party city. That said, there are still a decent number of options for late-night revelry, including stylish dance clubs and bohemian live-performance venues.

LONELY PLANET/GETTY IMAGES ©

Best Dance Clubs

Blob Club Trendy club with popular music theme nights (p96)

Flò Summer-only venue with themed lounge areas and a dance floor (p111)

Twice Club Stylish decor and a hip cocktail-quaffing crowd (p96)

Space Club Dancing, drinking and video-karaoke among a mixed, student-international crowd (p58)

YAB Over 30s head here on Thursdays, students on other nights (p46)

Best Music Clubs

Be Bop Music Club Retro venue featuring everything from Beatles cover bands to 1970s funk (p77)

Jazz Club The city's top jazz venue (p77)

Best Live Performance Venues

Le Murate Caffè Letterario Film screenings, book readings, live music and art exhibitions (p96)

Soul Kitchen DJs, live music and various hip happenings (p94)

Volume Music, art and DJs in an old hat-making workshop (p115)

Lion's Fountain Irish pub with live music (p95)

La Cité Vibrant alternative live-music space (p123)

Il Teatro del Sale Dinner followed by a performance of drama, music or comedy (p89)

☑ Top Tips

▶ Dress to impress for clubs – otherwise you may not gain entry

▶ Don't arrive before midnight – dance floors start to fill around 2am

▶ Some venues close between June and September

Best
Eating

Everyone eats well in Florence. Cooking is slow, seasonal and almost inevitably regional in its inspiration. Whether it be a snack from a street cart or a marathon meal in a Michelin-fêted restaurant, you can count on it being memorable and moreish.

RICHARD I'ANSON/GETTY IMAGES ©

Cafes

Florentines don't pause long for *colazione* (breakfast). Most make a quick dash into a bar or cafe for an espresso and *cornetto* (croissant) enjoyed standing at the bar. At *pranzo* (lunch), busy professionals will sometimes grab a quick snack at a cafe – usually a *panino* (sandwich) or *tramezzini* (the local version of a club sandwich) accompanied by a glass of wine or a coffee.

Trattorie, Osterie & Ristoranti

Champions of traditional Tuscan cuisine, these low-fuss eateries are greatly beloved in Florence. Popular for both *pranzo* and *cena* (dinner), they are often family run and usually excellent value for money. There's a fine line between an upmarket version of an *osteria* (casual tavern) or trattoria and a *ristorante*; the differences are that service is more formal in *ristoranti*, and the cuisine is more likely to be refined than rustic.

Enoteche

Enoteche (wine bars) are trending in today's Florence, popular for their focus on quality wine and light, seasonally driven dishes that are often described as 'Modern Tuscan'. Popular destinations for *aperitivi* (pre-dinner drinks accompanied by cocktail snacks), they are equally alluring for *pranzo* and *cena*.

Best Trattorie/ Osterie

L'Osteria di Giovanni Sensational food in convivial surrounds (p56)

Osteria Il Buongustai Cheap and tasty Tuscan lunches (p40)

Trattoria Mario Noisy, busy and totally brilliant trattoria near Mercato di San Lorenzo (p73)

Antica Trattoria da Tito An exemplar of traditional Tuscan cooking (p73)

Il Giova Everything a traditional Florentine eatery should be (p92)

Antico Noè Down-to-earth Tuscan fodder (p93)

Da Ruggero Family-run trattoria serving staunchly traditional food (p109)

La Casalinga One of Florence's cheapest and best trattorie (p119)

Osteria Bernardo, Pisa Perfect fusion of easy dining and gourmet excellence (p132)

Tamerò Hip version of a trattoria, specialising in pasta (p119)

Best Enoteche

Enoteca I Terzi, Siena Classy modern *enoteca* where the food is as impressive as the wine list (p147)

Cantinetta dei Verrazzano Focaccia straight from the oven and wine from Chianti's Verrazzano Estate (p42)

Francesco Vini Wine specialist with limited menu (p94)

Enoteca Fuori Porta Pastas, salads, snacks and a sensational wine list (p109)

Best Gelaterie

Grom, Florence & Siena Fantastic flavours, often made using organic ingredients (p43, p150)

Carabé Try a Sicilian-style *sorbetto* (sorbet) or *brioche* (ice-cream sandwich; p76)

Vivoli Long-standing favourite with large selection (p93)

Gelateria Santa Trìnita The perfect balance of sweetness and creaminess (p118)

Kopa Kabana, Siena Freshly made every day; particularly good fruit flavours (p150)

Best Ristoranti

Enoteca Pinchiorri The only restaurant in Tuscany with three Michelin stars (p93)

Il Santo Bevitore Modern Tuscan cuisine served in romantic surrounds (p119)

iO Osteria Personale Contemporary, creative rifts on Tuscan standards (p119)

Tre Cristi, Siena Specialises in fish (p148)

Ristorante Grotta Santa Caterina da Bagoga, Siena Traditional Tuscan palate pleasers (p147)

Best Sandwiches & Snacks

Gustapanino Fantastic *panini* washed down with a glass of wine (p119)

Mariano *Panini* and salads scoffed in a 13th-century cellar (p56)

'Ino Gourmet *panini* filled with locally sourced artisan ingredients (p43)

Il Crudo, Pisa Pocket-sized *pannineria* (sandwich shop) and *vineria* (wine bar; p132)

Best Pizzerie

Il Pizzaiuolo Thick-crust pizzas straight from a wood-fired oven (p95)

Pizzeria del' Osteria del Caffè Italiano Sometimes, the simplest is the best (p95)

Gustapizza No frills, but loads of flavour (p122)

Il Montino, Pisa Specialises in *cecina* (chickpea pizza; p132)

Best
Drinking

Welcome to one of Italy's best cafe and bar scenes. Visitors are spoiled for choice when it comes to choosing an atmospheric venue, and equally spoiled when it comes to the quality of the coffee, wine and food on offer.

BOB INGELHART/GETTY IMAGES ©

Cafes

Florence has cafes of every type – historic, hip, bohemian, cosy, and plenty with no frills. Most are bar/cafe hybrids, serving beer, wine and spirits as well as coffee, along with pastries in the morning and *panini* at lunch. Those located on piazzas often have terraces that are perfect places for whiling away an hour or so.

Locals usually drink their coffee standing at a cafe's *banco* (bar counter), where it is three to four times cheaper than a coffee ordered at a table.

Bars

You can drink at a bar at most times of the day, but most are at their best from 5pm (aka *aperitivo* time), when many places serve complimentary snacks with drinks.

Enoteche (wine bars) take pride in their selection of wines, and tend to concentrate on Tuscan tipples. Most offer antipasto platters of cheese, cured meats and *crostini* (toasts with various toppings) to eat, and some also offer light meals.

☑ Top Tips

▶ There is one cardinal rule: milky coffee such as cappuccino, caffe latte or latte macchiato is only ever drunk in the early morning – never, ever after a meal.

▶ A growing number of bars are building reputations for their *apericena,* an *aperitivo* buffet so copious it doubles as *cena* (dinner).

Best Historic Cafes

Caffè Rivoire The city's best location and its best hot chocolate, too (p160)

Gilli Serving excellent coffee and delicious cakes since 1733 (p45)

Rex Bar (p77)

Salza, Pisa Established in 1898; great for coffee or *aperitivo* (p133)

Caffè Fiorella, Siena Tiny space behind the Campo serving the city's best coffee (p149)

Best Hip Cafes

Gucci Museo Caffè Newspapers, iPads and art books to browse in Florence's most stylish cafe (p160)

Le Renaissance Café Arty hangout serving a sensational cappuccino (p158)

Caffè Giacosa Owned by fashion designer Roberto Cavalli (p158)

Cuculia Hybrid bookshop-cafe with an old-fashioned vibe (p123)

Sottobosco, Pisa Bohemian cafe during the day, laid-back music venue at night (p133)

Best Aperitivo

La Terrazza Snacks are meagre, but the view is sensational (p44)

Obikà Copious and good value, in superstylish surrounds (p42)

Sei Divino Happening scene from 5pm to 10pm (p56)

Kitsch American-styled bars popular with hipsters; lavish *aperitivo* spread (p95, p77)

Brac Vegetarian/vegan food (p93)

Keith, Pisa Terrace overlooking a Keith Haring mural (p133)

Enoteca I Terzi, Siena Choose from an extensive wine list and gourmet antipasti (p147)

Best Wine Bars

Le Volpi e l'Uva Impressive wine list and sensational antipasto choices (p110)

Il Santino Tranquil during the day, but heats up after 9pm (p122)

Vivanda Specialises in organic wine and gourmet antipasto plates (p122)

Coquinarius Friendly place with a refreshingly modern air and great food (p44)

Enoteca Italiana, Siena In the former munitions cellar and dungeon of a Medici fortress (p149)

Best Beer

Danny Rock Artisanal beer from around the globe (p95)

Lion's Fountain Guinness, Kilkenny and Harp (p95)

James Joyce Guinness on tap (p111)

Best
Activities

Though predominantly a destination for cultural tourists, Florence offers a reasonable number of opportunities for those who prefer to spend their holidays pursuing activities. Bike rides, tower climbs, guided tours and festivals are all in the mix, so take your pick and get started!

MARK BOLTON/GETTY IMAGES ©

Best Climbs

Campanile, Duomo 414 steps up Giotto's 85m belltower (p24)

Dome, Duomo 463 steps winding up the inside edge of Brunelleschi's extraordinary 114m dome (p24)

Torre d'Arnolfo 418 steps up the Palazzo Vecchio's 94m tower (p34)

Panorama del Facciatone, Siena 131 steps to the top of the never-finshed New Cathedral (p138)

Leaning Tower, Pisa 300-odd steps up the world-famous but decidedly wonky 56m tower (p127)

Torre del Mangia, Siena 102m high, with 500-odd steps (p145)

Torre Grossa, San Gimignano 154 steps and 54m high (p155)

Best Guided Tours

Corridoio Vasariano Walk in the steps of the Medicis from the Uffizi to Palazzo Pitti (p59)

Palazzo Vecchio Take the 'Secret Passages' or 'Experiencing the Palace First-Hand' tours (p34)

Giardino Torrigiani Let an Italian aristocrat show you his garden. (p105)

Duomo, Siena Join a tour of the cathedral run by Centro Guide Turistiche Siena e Provincia (p138)

Best Passeggiatas

City Wall, Lucca Along the path atop this Renaissance-era wall (p135)

Duomo to Piazza della Signoria An easy saunter between the cathedral and the city's most elegant square (p40)

Via de' Tornabuoni Florence's most glamorous shopping strip (p40)

Best Bike Rides

Fiesole to Florence A sunset ride guided by FiesoleBike (p81)

City wall, Lucca Hire a bike and use pedal power to circle the city (p135)

Best Festivals

Estate Fiesolana Music, theatre and cinema staged in a 1st-century-BC Roman theatre (p81)

Palio, Siena 90 seconds of high-octane excitement in Italy's famous horse race (p146)

Maggio Musicale Fiorentina This summertime extravaganza is the oldest music festival in Italy (p58)

Best
For Romance

MARK BOLTON/GETTY IMAGES ©

Few cities are as romantic as Florence. Come here to picnic in historic gardens, watch the sun set over the Arno or wander hand-in-hand through ancient cobbled streets. On the practical side, intimate restaurants with dinner tables for two are easy to find, as are luxury and designer hotels (many of these offering high levels of service and some with romantic accoutrements including panoramic terraces and tower suites).

Best Hotels

Antica Torre di Via de' Tornabuoni 1 Luxe rooms and a swoon-worthy terrace (p179)

Hotel L'O Moody wine bar and laid-back lounges (p179)

Palazzo Guadagni Hotel Dreamy loggia terrace overlooking Piazza Santo Spirito (p179)

Antica Dimora Johlea Quiet, opulently decorated B&B rooms (p179)

Palazzo Vecchietti Hopelessly romantic rooms, some with private terraces (p179)

Il Salviatino Luxury villa retreat just outside the city (p179)

Best Restaurants

Il Santo Bevitore Candlelit tables and Modern Tuscan cuisine (p119)

Obikà Sofa seating in an elegant, star-topped courtyard (p42)

Enoteca Pinchiorri Share a meal of a lifetime with your heart's desire (p93)

Best Cafes

Caffè Rivoire Stupendous view and old-fashioned service (p160)

Cuculia Complete with a tiny candlelit nook out back (p123)

Best Bars

La Terrazza Watch the sun set over the Arno while sipping *prosecco* (a type of sparkling wine; p44)

Il Santino Intimate space and a fantastic list of wine by the glass (p122)

Best
For Art

ALBORNO ANDREA/GETTY IMAGES ©

Florence has always embraced art and culture. Few artistic works remain from its days as a Roman colony, but plenty date from the Middle Ages, when the city first hit its artistic stride. Funded by medieval bankers, merchants and guilds, artists adorned the city's churches, *palazzi* (palaces) and public buildings with frescoes, sculptures and paintings of a quality never before encountered. This continued through the period now known as the Renaissance, bequeathing Florentines a truly extraordinary artistic heritage.

Medieval Art

The Middle Ages get a bad rap in the history books. This period may have been blighted by famines, plagues and wars, but it also saw the rise of civic culture in the Italian city-states, a phenomenon that led to an extraordinary flowering of painting and sculpture. When the Gothic style was imported from Northern Europe, local artists reworked it into a uniquely Tuscan form, creating works that were both sophisticated and elegant and that highlighted attention to detail, a luminous palette and increasingly refined techniques.

Renaissance Art

During the 15th century, painting overtook its fellow disciplines of sculpture and architecture and became the pre-eminent art form for the first time in the history of Western art. Painters experimented with perspective and proportion and took a new interest in realistic portraiture. Supported by wealthy patrons such as the Medicis, Florentine painters including Giotto di Bondone, Sandro Botticelli, Tommaso di Simone (Masaccio), Piero della Francesca, Fra' Angelico and Domenico Ghirlandaio were among many artistic innovators.

Best Frescoes

Basilica di Santa Maria Novella Ghirlandaio's panels in the Cappella Maggiore and Masaccio's *Trinity* (p50)

Cappella Brancacci Masaccio's *The Expulsion of Adam and Eve from Paradise* and *The Tribute Money* (p118)

Palazzo Medici-Riccardi Benozzo Gozzoli's *Adoration of the Magi* in the Cappella dei Magi (p71)

Museo di San Marco Fra Angelicos galore, including his *Annunciation* (p70)

Museo Civico, Siena Simone Martini's *Maestà* and Ambrogio Lorenzetti's *Allegories of Good and Bad Government* (p142)

Collegiata, San Gimignano Taddeo di Bartolo's *The Last Judgment* and

Uffizi Gallery (p30)

Domenico Ghirlandaio's Santa Fina panels (p155)

Duomo, Siena Bernardino Pinturicchio's *Life of Pius II* in the Libreria Piccolomini (p139)

Museo dell'Opera del Duomo, Siena Duccio di Buoninsegna's *Maestà* (p139)

Basilica di Santa Croce The Giotto panels in the Cappella Bardi and Cappella Peruzzi (p86)

Cenacolo di Sant'Apollonia Andrea del Castagno's *Last Supper* (p73)

Best Paintings

Uffizi Gallery Simply extraordinary collection including paintings by every major artist of the Italian Renaissance (p30)

Pinacoteca Nazionale, Siena Gothic masterpieces from the Sienese school (p145)

Museo Nazionale di San Matteo, Pisa Paintings from the medieval Tuscan school (p131)

Basilica di San Lorenzo Fra' Filippo Lippi's *Annunciation* (p66)

Palazzo Pitti Stellar collection of 16th- to 18th-century works in the Galleria Palatina (p100)

Best Sculptures

Museo del Bargello Donatello's two *David*s and early Michelangelos (p84)

Galleria dell'Accademia Michelangelo's *David* and his *Prigioni* ('Prisoners' or 'Slaves') group (p64)

Cappelle Medicee Michelangelo's *Dawn and Dusk*, *Night and Day* and *Madonna and Child* (p70)

Grande Museo del Duomo Ghiberti's *Door of Paradise* panels and Michelangelo's *La Pietà* (p29)

Duomo, Pisa Giovanni Pisano's pulpit (p127)

Battistero, Pisa Nicola Pisano's pulpit (p127)

Palazzo Vecchio Michelangelo's *Genius of Victory* in the Salone dei Cinquecento (p34)

Basilica di Santo Spirito Wooden crucifix attributed to Michelangelo (p118)

Best
For Families

If you're looking for a family-friendly destination, Florence, Pisa and Lucca all fit the bill. Your children might moan about the number of churches and museums on the itinerary, but they'll be quickly appeased by the delectable gelato (yay!), kid-friendly museums and outdoor activities on offer.

STREET LIFE/GETTY IMAGES ©

Best for Toddlers

Giardino di Boboli Statues, open spaces, hidden paths and a really weird 'face' sculpture (p104)

Piazza della Repubblica Ride a vintage carousel (p40)

Letizia Fiorini Charming shop selling traditional, hand-made puppets (p58)

Parco delle Cascine Open-air swimming pool and toddler-friendly playgrounds (p55)

Best for Bigger Kids

Palazzo Vecchio Climb the Torre d'Arnolfo and tour the palace's secret passages (p34)

Museo Galileo History of science museum with plenty of interactive displays (p38)

City wall, Lucca Hire a bike, pack a picnic and spend a day atop the wall (p135)

Duomo Climb up Giotto's *campanile* (bell tower) or into Brunelleschi's dome (p24)

Torre del Mangia, Siena Steep steps (lots of them) and awesome views (p145)

Galleria dell'Accademia Snigger at a really big, naked man (p64)

Leaning Tower, Pisa Climb it and take photographs of your kids holding it up (p127)

Best for Teenagers

FiesoleBike Take a sunset ride downhill from Fiesole to Florence (p81)

Gucci Museo Caffè Free iPad use in the cafe (p160)

☑ **Top Tips**

▶ Kids with EU passports who are under 18 receive free entry to many museums.

▶ Most streets are crowded and cobbled, so strollers aren't very useful – bring a backpack carrier instead.

Caffè Rivoire The hot chocolate hit of a lifetime (p160)

Survival Guide

Survival Guide

Before You Go

When to Go

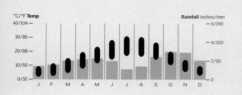

High Season (May, Jun, Sep, Oct): Perfect weather for travelling, but expect crowds and high accommodation prices.

Shoulder (Apr, Jul & Aug): Pleasant weather in April; July and August can be hot.

Low Season (Nov–Mar): Accommodation bargains abound, but many hotels and restaurants close.

Easter & Ferragosto (15 Aug): Popular with domestic tourists; book your accommodation well in advance.

Book Your Stay

➡ Accommodation options include hostels, family-run *pensioni* (guest houses), B&Bs, boutique hotels and luxury villa or *palazzo* (palace) hotels. It is always wise to book well ahead.

➡ Be sure to check hotel websites for special deals; in the low season, prices can drop by up to 50%.

➡ Hotels are nonsmoking by national law and many offer accommodation for mobility-impaired guests.

➡ In most parts of Tuscany there is a compulsory hotel occupancy tax (*tassa di soggiorno*) that is charged on top of your regular hotel bill and must generally be paid in cash. The exact amount depends on the type of place you stay in and the time of year, but as a rough guide expect to pay €1 per person per night in a one-star hotel or hostel, €2 in a B&B, €2 to €3 in a three-star hotel and €4 to €5 in a four- or five-star hotel.

Best Budget

Academy Hostel (www.academyhostel.eu) Cheap accommodation that doesn't compromise on comfort or cleanliness.

Hotel Scoti (www.hotelscoti.com) Splendid mix of old-fashioned charm and value for money located in a 16th-century *palazzo*.

Hotel Dali (www.hoteldali.com) Very friendly hotel with 10 spacious, homelike rooms.

Hotel Cestelli (www.hotelcestelli.com) Large rooms in a 12th-century *palazzo* close to fashionable Via de' Tornabuoni.

Best Midrange

Palazzo Guadagni Hotel (www.palazzoguadagni.com) Renaissance palace turned into a brilliant-value hotel complete with loggia terrace.

Hotel Torre Guelfa (www.hoteltorreguelfa.com) So historic it has its own 13th-century tower.

Hotel Davanzati (www.hoteldavanzati.it) Labyrinth of enchanting rooms, unexpected frescoes and modern comforts.

Antica Dimora Johlea (www.johanna.it) One of five historic and elegant B&B residences scattered around San Marco.

Best Top-End

Antica Torre di Via de' Tornabuoni 1 (www.tornabuoni1.com) Stylish, spacious and contemporary, with a stunning rooftop terrace.

Il Salviatino (www.salviatino.com) Luxury hotel hidden among cypress trees in the hills 3.5km east of Florence.

Hotel L'O (www.hotelorologioflorence.com) Elegant designer hotel in a wonderful location opposite the Basilica di Santa Maria Novella.

Palazzo Vecchietti (www.palazzovecchietti.com) Designer hotel in a 15th-century *palazzo*.

Arriving in Florence

☑ **Top Tip** For the best way to get to your accommodations, see p17.

Pisa International Airport

➡ Alternative name: Aeroporto Galileo Galilei.

➡ Tuscany's major air hub, linked with Florence's Stazione di Santa Maria Novella by train (€7.80, 1½ hours, at least hourly from 4.30am to 10.25pm).

➡ Hourly bus services to Florence are operated by Terravision (one way €4.99, 1¼ hours) – buy tickets on board or from the Terravision desk in the the arrival hall. The bus stop in Florence is in Piazza della Stazione, outside the train station.

Florence Airport

➡ Alternative names: Amerigo Vespucci; Peretola.

➡ A taxi to the *centro historico* (historical centre) costs a flat rate of €20 (€22 on Sundays and holidays, €23.30 between 10pm and 6am), plus €1 per bag.

➡ Volainbus shuttle buses (single/return €6/8, 25 minutes) travel to Piazza della Stazione every 30 minutes between 6am and 11.30pm.

Cutting Queues

In the high season, long queues are a fact of life at Florence's key museums. But for a fee of €3 per ticket (€4 for the Uffizi and Galleria dell'Accademia), tickets to nine *musei statali* (state museums) including the Uffizi, Galleria dell'Accademia, Palazzo Pitti, Museo del Bargello and the Cappelle Medicee can be reserved. In reality, the only museums where prebooking is recommended are the Uffizi and Accademia.

To organise your ticket, check the website or call **Firenze Musei** (Florence Museums; ☎ 055 29 48 83; www.firenzemusei.it; ⏰ telephone booking line 8.30am-6.30pm Mon-Fri, to 12.30pm Sat) or go to the ticketing desk at the rear of Chiesa di Orsanmichele or at every state museum in the city except the Accademia. Many hotels in Florence also prebook museum tickets for guests.

Stazione Santa Maria

➡ Most neighbourhoods are an easy walk from the main train station, which is located in Santa Maria Novella on the northwestern edge of the historical centre. A taxi within the centre will cost approximately €12.

Getting Around

Walking

☑ **Best for...** All exploration

➡ The narrow streets of the city centre are covered by a ZTL (*Zona a Traffico Limitato*; Limited Traffic Zone); motorised traffic is heavily restricted. Most people get around on foot.

Bus

☑ **Best for...** Day Trips to Fiesole, Siena and San Gimignano

➡ Buses to Fiesole (bus 7) leave from Piazza San Marco.

➡ Bus 13 runs uphill to Piazzale Michelangelo and the Basilica di San Miniato al Monte. It leaves from the ATAF bus stops near Stazione di Santa Maria Novella.

➡ Tickets are valid for 90 minutes and cost €1.20 when purchased from *tabacchi* (tobacconists) or the ATAF ticket & information office adjoining the train station, but cost €2 when purchased on board. Note that drivers don't give change.

➡ Buses to Siena and San Gimignano depart from the Sita Bus Station in Via Santa Caterina da Siena, off Piazza della Stazione.

Car & Motorcycle

☑ **Best for...** Day trips to Chianti

➡ The historical centres of Florence, Siena, Pisa, Lucca and San Gimignano are all covered by ZTLs; if you drive into them you risk a hefty fine. Plus, parking can be expensive and hard to access; you're better off using public transport.

Train

☑ **Best for...** Day trips to Pisa and Lucca

➡ Frequent services to Pisa, and less frequent to Lucca; check arrival and departure details at www.trenitalia.com.

➡ The historical centres of both Pisa and Lucca are an easy walk from their central train station.

Essential Information

Business Hours

☑ **Top Tip** Final entry to most museums is generally 30 minutes (sometimes one hour) before the official closing time. We have cited the time for last entry in most reviews.

In this book, we include opening times for most individual businesses. As a general rule:

Banks 8.30am to 1.30pm and 3.30pm to 4.30pm Monday to Friday

Bars & pubs 10am to 1am

Cafes 7.30am to 8pm

Nightclubs 10pm to late

Pharmacies 9am to 12.30pm and 3.30pm to 7pm Monday to Friday, 9am to 12.30pm Saturday and Sunday

Restaurants 12.30pm to 2.30pm and 7.30pm to 10pm

Shops 9am to 1pm and 3.30pm to 7.30pm (or 4pm to 8pm) Monday to Saturday

Discount Cards

The **Firenze Card** (www.firenzecard.it; €72) is valid for 72 hours and covers admission to 72 museums, villas and gardens in Florence as well as unlimited use of public transport. Buy it online (and collect upon arrival in Florence) or in Florence at tourist offices or at the ticketing desks of the Uffizi (Entrance 2), Palazzo Pitti, Palazzo Vecchio, Museo del Bargello, Cappella Brancacci, Basilica Santa Maria Novella and Giardini Bardini. If you're an EU citizen your card also covers under-18s travelling with you.

Electricity

120V/60Hz

230V/50Hz

Emergency

Ambulance (free from landline) ☎118

Local police (free from landline) ☎113

Emergency from mobile phone ☎112

Money

Currency The euro.

ATMs *Bancomats* (ATM machines) are widespread.

Credit cards International credit and debit cards can be used at any *bancomat* displaying the appropriate sign. Cards are also good for most hotels, restaurants, shops, supermarkets and tollbooths.

Money changers Change money in banks, at the post office or in a *cambio* (exchange office); post offices and banks tend to offer the best rates.

Tipping Many locals don't tip waiters, but most visitors leave 10% to 15% if there's no service charge. Bellhops usually expect €1 to €2 per bag. In taxis, round the fare up to the nearest euro.

Public Holidays

New Year's Day (Capodanno or Anno Nuovo) 1 January

Epiphany (Epifania or Befana) 6 January

Anniversary of the Unification of Italy (Anniversario dell'Unità d'Italia) 17 March

Easter Sunday (Domenica di Pasqua) March/April

Easter Monday (Pasquetta or Lunedì dell'Angelo) March/April

Liberation Day (Giorno della Liberazione) 25 April

Labour Day (Festa del Lavoro) 1 May

Republic Day (Festa della Repubblica) 2 June

Feast of the Assumption (Assunzione or Ferragosto) 15 August

All Saints' Day (Ognissanti) 1 November

Feast of the Immaculate Conception (Immaculata Concezione) 8 December

Christmas Day (Natale) 25 December

Boxing Day (Festa di Santo Stefano) 26 December

Telephone

Mobile Phones

➡ Italy uses GSM 900/1800, compatible with the rest of Europe and Australia but not with North American GSM 1900 or the Japanese system.

➡ For a local prepaid SIM card, you must register with a telecommunications provider such as TIM, Vodafone or Wind; all have a shops in major Tuscan towns. Accounts take about 24 hours to activate (you'll need to show your passport). Costs are as low as €20 (some with €10 worth of calls on the card) and *ricarica* (prepaid minutes) can then be purchased from provider shops, *tabacchi* or newsstands. If you have an internet-enabled phone, be sure to turn off your data roaming function when you're not using it, as it devours credit.

➡ Mobile-phone numbers begin with a three-digit prefix such as 330.

Phone Codes

Country code 39

International access code 00

Money-Saving Tips

➡ The *duomo* (cathedral) complexes in Florence, Siena and Pisa all offer money-saving combined passes.

➡ EU passport holders aged under 18 and over 65 get into many museums for free, and EU citizens aged 18 to 25 pay half-price. Have your ID with you at all times.

Area codes Begin with 0 and consist of up to four digits; this is an integral part of the telephone number and must always be dialled.

Toilets

Public toilets aren't common; take advantage of facilities in hotels, restaurants, cafes and museums.

Tourist Information

→ There are tourist offices at both Florence and Pisa airports. In Florence, there are offices in Via Cavour, next to the Palazzo Medici-Riccardi; on Piazza della Stazione, opposite the train station; and in the Loggia del Bigallo, opposite the *duomo* (cathedral).

→ For tourist information check **Firenze Turismo** (www.firenzeturismo.it), **Pisa Tourism** (www.pisaunica-terra.it), www.luccatourist.it for Lucca and **Terre**

di **Siena** (www.terresiena.it) for Siena and San Gimignano.

Visas

→ Italy is one of 26 member countries of the Schengen Convention, under which EU countries (except Bulgaria, Cyprus, Ireland, Romania and the UK) plus Iceland, Liechtenstein, Norway and Switzerland have abol-

ished permanent checks at common borders.

→ Legal residents of one Schengen country do not require a visa for another. Residents of 28 non-EU countries, including Australia, Brazil, Canada, Israel, Japan, New Zealand and the USA, do not require visas for tourist visits of up to 90 days.

→ For more information, visit www.esteri.it.

Dos & Don'ts

→ **Greetings** Shake hands, make eye contact and say *buongiorno* (good morning/afternoon), *buonasera* (good evening) or *piacere* (pleased to meet you).

→ **Polite language** Say *mi scusi* to attract attention or to say 'I'm sorry', *grazie (mille)* to say 'thank you (very much)', *per favore* to say 'please', *prego* to say 'you're welcome' or 'please, after you' and *permesso* if you need to push past someone in a crowd.

→ **Cafes** Don't hang around at an espresso bar; drink your coffee and go. It's called espresso for a reason.

→ **Churches** Never intrude on a mass or service.

Language

Standard Italian is taught and spoken throughout Italy. Regional dialects are an important part of identity in many parts of the country, but you'll have no trouble being understood anywhere if you stick to standard Italian, which we've also used in this chapter.

The sounds used in spoken Italian can all be found in English. If you read our pronunciation guides as if they were English, you'll be understood. The stressed syllables are indicated with italics. Note that *ai* is pronounced as in 'aisle', *ay* as in 'say', *ow* as in 'how', *dz* as the 'ds' in 'lids', and that *r* is a strong and rolled sound.

To enhance your trip with a phrasebook, visit **lonelyplanet.com**. Lonely Planet iPhone phrasebooks are available through the Apple App store.

Basics

Hello.
Buongiorno.   bwon·*jor*·no

Goodbye.
Arrivederci.   a·ree·ve·*der*·chee

How are you?
Come sta?   *ko*·me sta

Fine. And you?
Bene. E Lei?   *be*·ne e lay

Please.
Per favore.   per fa·*vo*·re

Thank you.
Grazie.   *gra*·tsye

Excuse me.
Mi scusi.   mee *skoo*·zee

Sorry.
Mi dispiace.   mee dees·*pya*·che

Yes./No.
Sì./No.   see/no

I don't understand.
Non capisco.   non ka·*pee*·sko

Do you speak English?
Parla inglese?   *par*·la een·*gle*·ze

Eating & Drinking

I'd like ...   *Vorrei ...*   vo·*ray* ..

a coffee   *un caffè*   oon ka·*fe*

a table   *un tavolo*   oon ta·*vo*·lo

the menu   *il menù*   eel me·*noo*

two beers   *due birre*   *doo*·e *bee*·re

What would you recommend?
Cosa mi consiglia?   *ko*·za mee kon·*see*·lya

Enjoy the meal!
Buon appetito!   bwon a·pe·*tee*·to

That was delicious!
Era squisito!   *e*·ra skwee·*zee*·to

Cheers!
Salute!   sa·*loo*·te

Please bring the bill.
Mi porta il conto, per favore?   mee *por*·ta eel *kon*·to per fa·*vo*·re

Shopping

I'd like to buy ...
Vorrei comprare ...   vo·*ray* kom·*pra*·re ...

I'm just looking.
Sto solo guardando.   sto *so*·lo gwar·*dan*·do

How much is this?
Quanto costa   kwan·to kos·ta
questo?   kwe·sto

It's too expensive.
È troppo caro/   e tro·po ka·ro/
cara. (m/f)   ka·ra

Emergencies

Help!
Aiuto!   a·yoo·to

Call the police!
Chiami la   kya·mee la
polizia!   po·lee·tsee·a

Call a doctor!
Chiami un   kya·mee oon
medico!   me·dee·ko

I'm sick.
Mi sento male.   mee sen·to ma·le

I'm lost.
Mi sono perso/   mee so·no per·so/
persa. (m/f)   per·sa

Where are the toilets?
Dove sono i   do·ve so·no ee
gabinetti?   ga·bee·ne·tee

Time & Numbers

What time is it?
Che ora è?   ke o·ra e

It's (two) o'clock.
Sono le (due).   so·no le (doo·e)

morning	*mattina*	ma·tee·na
afternoon	*pomeriggio*	po·me·ree·jo
evening	*sera*	se·ra
yesterday	*ieri*	ye·ree
today	*oggi*	o·jee
tomorrow	*domani*	do·ma·nee

1	*uno*	oo·no
2	*due*	doo·e
3	*tre*	tre
4	*quattro*	kwa·tro
5	*cinque*	cheen·kwe
6	*sei*	say
7	*sette*	se·te
8	*otto*	o·to
9	*nove*	no·ve
10	*dieci*	dye·chee
100	*cento*	chen·to
1000	*mille*	mee·le

Transport & Directions

Where's ...?
Dov'è ...?   do·ve ...

What's the address?
Qual'è   kwa·le
l'indirizzo?   leen·dee·ree·tso

Can you show me (on the map)?
Può mostrarmi   pwo mos·trar·mee
(sulla pianta)?   (soo·la pyan·ta)

At what time does the ... leave?
A che ora   a ke o·ra
parte ...?   par·te

Does it stop at ...?
Si ferma a ...?   see fer·ma a ...

How do I get there?
Come ci si   ko·me chee see
arriva?   a·ree·va

bus	*l'autobus*	low·to·boos
ticket	*un biglietto*	oon bee·lye·to
timetable	*orario*	o·ra·ryo
train	*il treno*	eel tre·no

Index

See also separate subindexes for:

Eating p189
Drinking p189
Entertainment p190
Shopping p190

Sights p000
Map Pages **p000**

Sights p000
Map Pages p000

Beh领 the Scenes

Send Us Your Feedback

We love to hear from travellers – your comments help make our books better. We read every word, and we guarantee that your feedback goes straight to the authors. Visit **lonelyplanet.com/contact** to submit your updates and suggestions.

Note: We may edit, reproduce and incorporate your comments in Lonely Planet products such as guidebooks, websites and digital products, so let us know if you don't want your comments reproduced or your name acknowledged. For a copy of our privacy policy visit lonelyplanet.com/privacy.

Our Readers

Many thanks to the travellers who used the last edition and wrote to us with helpful hints, useful advice and interesting anecdotes:

Marina Hadjiyanni, Elizabeth Hill, Jasper Lorentzen, Anastasia Mujortova, Joachim Selvais

Virginia's Thanks

Love and thanks to my partner and travelling companion, Peter Handsaker. Thanks also to Ilaria Crescioli, Susanna Scali, Alberto Peruzzini, Roberta Vichi, Sigrid Fuchs, Chiara Ponzuoli, Luigina Benci and Fulvia in San Gimignano.

Nicola's Thanks

Grazie mille to everyone who helped me delve deep into the Tuscan heart: Krista Ricchi (@allafiorentina), Marquis Vanni and Susanna Torrigiani Malaspina (what a beautiful garden), Guido Manfredi (no farm is finer), Alessandro Gargani (New York to Florence), Antje d'Almeida (for directing me to CLET), Roberta Romoli, and Freya Middleton (guide extraordinaire); husband Matthias and our trilingual tribe of fearless young road-trippers.

Acknowledgments

Cover photograph: Battistero di San Giovanni, Florence/Maurizio Rellini/4 Corners ©.

This Book

This guidebook was commissioned in Lonely Planet's London office, and produced by the following:

Commissioning Editors Joe Bindloss, Helena Smith **Coordinating Editors** Fionnuala Twomey, Jeanette Wall **Senior Cartographer** Valentina Kremenchutskaya **Coordinating Layout Designer** Clara Monitto **Managing Editors** Brigitte Ellemor, Bruce Evans **Senior Editors** Catherine Naghten, Karyn Noble **Managing Layout Designer** Jane Hart **Cover Research** Naomi Parker **Internal Image Research** Aude Vauconsant **Language Content** Annelies Mertens, Branislava Vladisavljevic **Thanks to** Ryan Evans, Larissa Frost, Genesys India, Jouve India, Andi Jones, Wayne Murphy, Trent Paton, Kerrianne Southway, Gerard Walker

OUR WRITERS

Virginia Maxwell

Based in Australia, Virginia spends part of every year in Italy indulging her passions for history, art, architecture, food and wine. She is the coordinating author of Lonely Planet's *Florence & Tuscany* guidebook, wrote the Tuscany chapter in *Italy,* and covers other parts of the country for the *Western Europe* guidebook. Though reticent to nominate a favourite Italian destination (arguing that they're all wonderful), she tends to nominate Florence if pressed.
http://www.lonelyplanet.com/members/virginiamaxwell

Nicola Williams

A British writer and editorial consultant, Nicola has lived on the southern shore of Lake Geneva for over a decade. Thankfully for her Italianate soul, it is an easy hop through the Mont Blanc Tunnel to Italy where she has spent years eating her way around and revelling in its extraordinary art and landscape. Nicola has worked on numerous Lonely Planet titles, including *Florence & Tuscany* and *Italy*. She blogs at tripalong.wordpress.com and tweets @Tripalong.
http://www.lonelyplanet.com/members/nicolawilliams

Published by Lonely Planet Publications Pty Ltd
ABN 36 005 607 983
3rd edition – Feb 2014
ISBN 978 1 74220 210 5
© Lonely Planet 2014 Photographs © as indicated 2014
10 9 8 7 6 5 4 3
Printed in China